LAW OF THE LAND

A Practical Legal Guide for Tourists and Business Travelers

The UK

By Michael L. Moore Esq.

Edited by Ally Knez-Siddique

Cover Design: Kristina Conatser

Published by: Law of the Land Publishing LLC

ISBN: 978-1-964870-12-0

DEDICATION

This book is dedicated to the memory of my late older brother, Kenneth Lee Moore, whose tragic murder at 15 years of age inspired me to write this series of books.

This book is also dedicated to my parents, John Henry Moore, and Edna Mae Moore, whose tremendous parenting skills kept me focused on the important things in life: being reverent, getting educated, and prioritizing family.

Finally, this book is dedicated to my beautiful family, my wife Royellen, my son AJ, and my daughter Karla. They inspire me every single day to be kind, patient, and compassionate.

IN LOVING MEMORY OF:

Belinda Joyce Moore Moss—my beautiful and wonderful sister, who supported me in every positive thing that I ever attempted to do.

Michael Eugene Baker—my dedicated and loyal friend and brother, who always wanted the very best for me.

Sylvia Joyce Hill—my eldest sister, who had a beautiful spirit and was like a second mother to me.

LAW OF THE LAND®
PUBLISHING for Tourists & Business Travelers

Travel smart. Stay legal. Stay safe.®

From local laws to medical guides we've got you covered world wide in one digital platform.

Travel Safe Anywhere
3 MONTHS FREE TRIAL

SCAN QR code
for more info

PREFACE

My introduction to the justice system came when I was only 10 years old. My 15-year-old brother was murdered with a butcher knife by a 19-year-old in a simple argument over a torn shirt. I was devastated by his death and sought retribution for his fate that never came. The woman was initially charged with second degree murder, but after plea negotiations, she was convicted of manslaughter and sentenced to only five years in a youthful offender school and ordered to undergo psychiatric care. That was it. Nothing more. The judicial system had run its course.

My family knew nothing about the justice system, and we did not have the tools to advocate for ourselves. No one provided us with a written source to reference for guidance through this process. There was no easily accessible, easy to understand, definitive source to educate ourselves about the legal system that we suddenly and unexpectedly found ourselves immersed in after being victimized by such a violent criminal act.

As I got older, finished college, law school, and ultimately started practicing law, it became clear to me that most people are not knowledgeable about the law or how the judicial process works. If most people are uninformed here in the United States regarding the law and the legal process, how would they fare when in other countries? I realized that tourists and businesspeople who travel internationally needed access to information on how to navigate the legal system in other countries!

For many years, there has been considerable media attention focused on international travelers experiencing legal difficulties while traveling abroad. Most of these news stories gained attention in the United States and abroad because they involved American citizens facing punishment that was considered "unconventional" and "harsh" by United States' legal standards. I recall a news story in 1994 regarding Michael Fay, a young American male, who had broken the law in Singapore. He was convicted and sentenced to be caned and or whipped publicly. While the United States Government weighed in on the inappropriate and cruel nature of the punishment, the young American was beaten because he had been convicted under Singapore law.

Similarly, in recent years, international news stories have garnered headlines regarding foreign travelers and their issues with the laws of countries that were not their own. Amanda Knox, an American woman, was accused of murdering her roommate in Italy in 2007 and spent almost four years in an Italian prison before being definitively acquitted by the Supreme Court of Cassatio. Kenneth Bae, an American citizen, was arrested in North Korea in 2012 and was convicted for hostile acts against the communist country. He was sentenced to 15 years hard labor but was released in 2014 after efforts by the U.S. State Department. More recently, United States Basketball Star, Brittany Griner was arrested in February 2022 at a Moscow airport on drug-related charges and detained for nearly 10 months, spending much of that time in prison. Her plight unfolded at the same time Russia invaded Ukraine and further heightened tensions between Russia and the United States, ending only after she was freed in exchange for a notorious Russian arms dealer.

It was in 1994 that another personal tragic event occurred that finally inspired me to write these series of books. A dear friend and also client of mine was brutally murdered while on his second honeymoon in Jamaica. News of his murder shocked me and our local community. The legal hurdles his family had to overcome to see that justice was properly dispensed far away from home, in another country, with an entirely different set of criminal procedural rules and laws, was difficult to navigate.

As I was my friend's attorney at the time of his death, his family asked that I act as their "legal liaison" to the Jamaican Prosecutor's Office and to the Jamaican Police Department. I participated in multiple police interviews with my client's widow because she was the primary witness to his murder. As a former prosecuting attorney, I was also allowed by the Court, as a professional courtesy, to sit at the prosecutor's table to consult with the prosecuting attorney during trial. What I observed about the Jamaican trial process from a front row seat was compelling enough to cause me to seriously consider educating the "world" regarding what to expect and how to act appropriately when faced with legal issues while traveling abroad.

One of the realities in life is that, regardless of what country you are in, it is never a pleasant experience to run afoul of the law and be forced to accept that someone else will be making a decision about your pecuniary, proprietary, or penal interests (your money, your property, or your freedom).

It is important to know what the laws are, how they apply to you, and how to navigate the legal system if you are charged with a crime. It is also very helpful to know what resources are available to you if you are the victim of a criminal act. At the end of the day, an "ounce of prevention is worth a pound of cure," so the more knowledge you have, the more ammunition you possess, and the more likely you will have a positive outcome.

If you are traveling to the UK, the first thing you should pack is a copy of this book! The helpful information and tips contained in this volume will provide a great starting point for knowing what to do (and not to do!) when you arrive at your destination and will help ensure that you have a wonderful vacation or business trip unmarred by tangles with the law.

TABLE OF CONTENTS

INTRODUCTION

INTRODUCTION

As a practicing attorney for over 34 years, I have encountered numerous clients who travel often, but are unaware of the laws of the land they are traveling to.

Therefore, many years ago, I decided to write a series of books that would explain the laws of specific countries. My focus was to explain the laws that may affect travelers in a straightforward manner, without all of the legal language that is sometimes hard for even seasoned attorneys to understand.

About This Book

The aim of this book is simple. It provides you, the traveler, with a simple, easy to read book that will provide a basic legal guide that explains the law in the country that you are about to visit. It is not intended to educate you on ALL of the laws in a given country. The goal is to provide you with the details of the most common legal and safety issues faced by tourists and business travelers.

I have also provided context with background information on places not to visit, statistics on the country and prevention measures you should take to safeguard your legal and physical safety. Knowledge is a powerful thing and knowing how to stay out of trouble (or how to get out of it!) is important for everyone who travels.

This *Law of The Land/The UK* book simply helps you become more informed about your legal rights, responsibilities, and obligations in a wide range of subject areas.

Last, but not least, this book does NOT purport to offer legal advice. It does, however, provide the information you need to stay safe, follow the law and navigate around legal difficulties. However, if you do face legal difficulties, the information in this book will provide you with a starting point for solving the problem and obtaining legal assistance should it be required.

Hypotheticals Used Throughout This Book

From time to time throughout this book, I will explain the law to readers by using hypothetical scenarios. These hypotheticals will be marked by an icon that will be explained in further detail as you read on.

How This Book is Organized

CHAPTER 1: **About the UK.** This chapter will provide you with a brief overview about the UK and its history. It also addresses Visa requirements, monetary advice, and the best times to visit.

CHAPTER 2: **Customs.** This chapter will provide information on what to expect when entering the UK. It will also explain what restricted and prohibited items are when entering the UK along with custom's regulations.

CHAPTER 3: **Crime in the UK.** This chapter provides an overview of the history of crime in the UK and steps that the UK's officials have taken to curb the high rate of crime.

CHAPTER 4: **Criminal Law Violations.** This chapter will provide information on drug offenses, penalties, true events and questions and answers.

CHAPTER 5: **Alcohol-Related Offenses.** This chapter will provide key points regarding the sale, consumption, and regulations of alcohol use in the UK.

CHAPTER 6: **Firearm & Ammunition Offenses.** This chapter will provide key points regarding the possession of firearms and ammunition in the UK.

CHAPTER 7: **Prostitution.** This chapter provides an overview of the history of prostitution in the UK, laws and penalties, prostitution practices, sex trafficking, sex tourism, health in the UK, tips to avoid being hassled, a Law of the Land Hypothetical, and the current situation on prostitution in the UK.

CHAPTER 8: **LGBTQ.** This chapter will provide information regarding the acceptance of LGBTQ people in the UK and the laws surrounding homosexuality.

CHAPTER 9: **Sexually Motivated/Violent Crimes.** This chapter will provide an overview of sexually related crimes in the UK.

CHAPTER 10: **Arrested in the UK.** This chapter will provide information on what to do if you are arrested in the UK.

CHAPTER 11: **Jails vs. Prisons: Conditions & Culture.** This chapter will provide information on the conditions and culture of the UK's Jails and Prisons.

CHAPTER 12: **Helping a Friend or Relative Imprisoned in the UK.** This chapter will provide information on how you can assist a friend or relative imprisoned in the UK.

CHAPTER 13: **The Administration of Justice.** This chapter will provide information on the UK's Legal System.

CHAPTER 14: **Crime Victim Assistance.** This chapter will provide information on crime victim assistance along with providing safety tips.

CHAPTER 15: **Police.** This chapter will provide information on the UK Police and how to report a crime.

CHAPTER 16: **How to Get Legal Help in the UK.** This chapter will provide information regarding how to obtain legal assistance for travelers to the UK.

CHAPTER 17: **Medical Facilities & Hospitals.** This chapter will provide information about how to obtain medical care while visiting the UK.

CHAPTER 18: **Driving in the UK.** This chapter will provide information on driving in the UK, it's traffic rules, and road safety tips.

CHAPTER 19: **Nude Beaches and Clothing-Optional Resorts.** This chapter will provide an overview of nude beaches and clothing-optional resorts in the UK, and the legality and safety of visiting nude beaches in the UK.

CHAPTER 20: **Unusual Laws.** This chapter will provide information on some Unusual Laws in the UK, and penalties and fines.

CHAPTER 21: **Traveling Safely.** This chapter will provide information on women traveling alone, crime prevention for families, safety notes for all travelers, and overall advice.

CHAPTER 22: **Tourist Taxation.** This chapter will provide information on taxes that tourists are required to pay in the UK.

CHAPTER 23: **Long-Term Stays.** This chapter will provide an overview of the consequences for overstaying your visit to the UK.

CHAPTER 24: **Civil Litigation.** This chapter will provide information about the civil litigation process in the UK.

CHAPTER 25: **Other Things to Know.** This chapter will provide information on the harassment of tourists, travel and safety, and other practical tips.

CHAPTER 26: **Quick Reference Guide.** This chapter is a quick way to get information. It is a condensed version of the chapters in this book.

Emergency/Important Contact Numbers in the UK

Useful British Phrases

Glossary

Icons Used in this Book

What do those pictures throughout the book mean? See below:

 **WARNING**: This icon flags information about things you should **avoid** while visiting the UK. Heed the advice next to this icon to avoid legal perils.

 **REMEMBER**: This icon flags noteworthy information that you **shouldn't forget.**

 **HELPFUL TIPS**: This icon flags information that will help you when entering the UK, relates to a legal situation, or refers to resources available while visiting the UK.

 **TECHNICAL INFORMATION**: This icon flags technical aspects of the law. If you are faced with a legal problem, and you want to learn more about the law involved, this information can be helpful.

 **ADDITIONAL INFORMATION**: This icon points to the location of additional information available on the internet.

 **HYPOTHETICAL**: This icon points to hypothetical scenarios to illustrate possible legal problems and the outcome.

 **QUESTIONS**: This icon points to questions and answers throughout the book.

 **TRUE STORY**: This icon points to true events throughout the book.

Where to Go From Here

If you have a specific question about the law in the UK as it relates to a particular area, just turn to the chapter that addresses that issue, or turn to the Quick Reference Guide. You can also read the book from cover to cover to obtain a more comprehensive understanding of the UK laws and resources available should you find yourself in a legal predicament while visiting.

 **Disclaimer:** While the recommendations in this book primarily address U.S. citizens, the information is relevant and applicable to citizens of any country.

ABOUT THE UK

ABOUT THE UK

About the UK[1]

The United Kingdom (UK) is an island nation in **northwestern Europe**, consisting of four countries: **England, Scotland, Wales, and Northern Ireland**. It covers an area of 243,610 square kilometers (94,058 square miles), with England being the largest. Surrounded by the Atlantic Ocean, the North Sea, the English Channel, and the Irish Sea, the UK has a unique geographic and cultural identity.

As of 2023, the UK has a population of around **67 million people**. England, the most populous country, is home to about 56 million people, while Scotland, Wales, and Northern Ireland have smaller populations. The UK has a rich **historical legacy**, once at the center of the British Empire, which helped shape global politics, trade, and culture. This influence continues to resonate on the world stage today.

The UK is renowned for its **contributions to literature**, with iconic authors like **William Shakespeare, Jane Austen**, and **Charles Dickens**. Its **music scene** is legendary, producing globally influential bands such as **The Beatles, The Rolling Stones**, and **Queen**. The UK is also home to **famous landmarks** like **Big Ben, Buckingham Palace**, and **Stonehenge**, attracting millions of tourists each year.

---

1   https://www.britannica.com/place/United-Kingdom

The British monarchy is a key symbol of tradition, continuity, and national identity. Although the monarch no longer has political power, the Royal Family remains an important figurehead. In education, the UK boasts world-class universities such as Oxford and Cambridge, known for their academic excellence. Despite leaving the European Union in 2020 through Brexit, the UK continues to play a **central role in international affairs** and remains a cultural, historical, and economic powerhouse.

The history of the UK spans many centuries and is shaped by key events and shifts. Following the fall of the Roman Empire in the fifth century, **Anglo-Saxon** and **Viking tribes** settled in what is now England, while Scotland and Wales followed their own **Celtic traditions**. In 1066, **William the Conqueror** invaded England, establishing Norman rule and centralizing power. By the sixteenth century, under **Henry VIII**, England broke from the Catholic Church, creating the Church of England. In 1707, the **Union of England and Scotland** formed Great Britain, and by the nineteenth century, Britain controlled a vast empire across the globe. **Ireland** joined the union in 1801, but after the **Irish War of Independence**, the majority of Ireland became independent in 1922, leaving Northern Ireland part of the UK.

The UK played a major role in both **World Wars**, which weakened the British Empire. After World War II, the UK began decolonizing, granting independence to many former colonies. The **National Health Service (NHS)** was created in 1948, and the country rebuilt its economy. In the late twentieth century, the UK joined the **European Union** in 1973 but officially left in 2020 following **Brexit**. Despite its smaller empire, the UK remains a key global player in politics, culture, and economics.

The Capital

London, the capital of the UK, is **one of the world's most iconic and influential cities.** Located on the **River Thames**, it has a history spanning over 2,000 years, starting as a Roman settlement called Londinium. Today, it is the **largest city in the UK**, with a population of around **9 million people**. London is a global hub for finance, home to institutions like the **London Stock Exchange** and the **Bank of England**. The city also plays a central role in British politics, housing key landmarks like the **Houses of Parliament**, **Buckingham Palace**, and **10 Downing Street**, where the UK's government is based.

Culturally, London is renowned for its **world-class museums, theaters**, and **galleries**, such as the British Museum and the Tate Modern, as well as its **vibrant theater scene** in the West End. The city is also home to **prestigious universities** like Imperial College and University College London. With **iconic landmarks** such as **Big Ben**, the **Tower of London, Buckingham Palace** and the **London Eye**, alongside lush parks like Hyde Park, London blends history, culture, and modernity. With its rich history, diverse population, and pivotal role in global affairs, London is more than just the capital of the UK; it stands as a symbol of British identity and a major force in the world's cultural, political, and economic spheres.

The People

The people of the UK are known for their rich diversity, shaped by a long history of immigration, colonization, and cultural exchange. The majority of the population is of **British descent**, with English people making up the largest group, followed by Scots, Welsh, and Northern Irish. The UK has a **significant immigrant population**, particularly in cities like London, Birmingham, and Manchester, which contributes to a **multicultural society**. People from countries like India, Pakistan, the Caribbean, and various European nations have made the UK their home, enriching the country's cultural landscape with diverse traditions, languages, and religions.

Language

The primary language spoken in the UK is **English**, which is also one of the most widely spoken languages in the world. It serves as the **official language** and is used in government, business, education, and daily life. In addition to English, the UK has several regional and minority languages. **Welsh** is spoken in Wales and has official status, while **Scottish Gaelic** is used by some communities in Scotland. **Irish** is spoken in parts of Northern Ireland, particularly in rural areas.

Due to the UK's multicultural population, many other languages are spoken, including **Punjabi**, **Urdu**, **Polish**, and **Arabic**, reflecting the diverse immigrant communities. While English is the dominant language, the UK's linguistic landscape is rich and varied, with different accents and dialects found across regions, such as Cockney, Geordie, and Scouse in England, and distinct Scottish and Welsh accents.

Religion

Religion in the UK is diverse, with **Christianity** being the largest and historically dominant faith. The majority of Christians in the UK belong to the **Church of England** (Anglican), though there are also significant communities of **Roman Catholics**, **Methodists**, and **Baptists**. They play a role in the UK's cultural and national identity, with many holidays, traditions, and rituals rooted in Christian history.

However, the UK is also home to a growing number of other religions due to its multicultural population. **Islam** is the second-largest religion, with a significant Muslim community, particularly in cities like London and Birmingham. Other notable religious groups include **Hinduism**, **Sikhism**, and **Judaism**, reflecting the UK's history of immigration from countries such as India, Pakistan, and various parts of Europe. There is also a sizable **non-religious** population, with many people identifying as **atheists** or **agnostics**, reflecting the country's increasingly secular outlook. Overall, the UK is known for its religious tolerance, with freedom of worship protected by law, and a wide variety of beliefs coexisting peacefully within the society.

Affordability

The affordability of living in the UK can **vary significantly** depending on the region, lifestyle, and specific needs of individuals or families. Generally, the UK is considered **moderately expensive**, especially in major cities like **London**, where housing costs are **notably high**. Rent, property prices, and general living expenses in London and the surrounding areas are some of the highest in Europe. However, costs tend to be **lower** in other parts of the UK, particularly in the **north of**

England, **Wales**, and **Scotland**, where housing is more affordable, and daily expenses may be lower.

In terms of **food, transportation**, and **utilities**, the UK is relatively affordable compared to some other Western European countries. Groceries and public transportation are reasonably priced, though they can add up, particularly in larger cities. The UK has a relatively high cost of living overall, but there are ways to manage expenses by choosing more affordable areas to live, cutting back on discretionary spending, and shopping smartly.

For those on a budget, living outside of the more expensive cities, taking advantage of **public services** like the **NHS** (National Health Service), and seeking **budget accommodation** can make the UK more affordable

Additionally, the cost of education, healthcare, and utilities is subsidized for residents, which helps mitigate some of the overall expenses. However, for those living in London or other high-cost urban centers, maintaining an affordable lifestyle can be challenging without a high income.

The UK, the Basics

How to Get There?

Getting to the UK is relatively straightforward, thanks to its well-connected network of international airports and airlines. The UK's largest and busiest airport is **London Heathrow**, located just west of the capital. It serves as a major hub for flights coming in from all over the world, making it the most common point of entry for travelers. Just a bit further south is **London Gatwick**, another major international gateway, offering a wide range of flights, especially to destinations in Europe, North America, and Asia. Other notable airports include **Manchester Airport**, which is the busiest airport outside of London, **London Stansted**, known for budget airlines, and **London Luton**, which also caters to low-cost carriers.

Several airlines operate within the UK, both for domestic and international flights:

1. **British Airways:** The UK's national carrier, British Airways, is a major player in international travel and offers flights to numerous global destinations from its hubs at Heathrow and Gatwick.

2. **EasyJet:** A popular low-cost carrier, EasyJet offers budget-friendly flights across Europe and is based at several UK airports, including Gatwick, Luton, and Manchester.

3. **Ryanair:** Another major low-cost airline, Ryanair operates extensively within Europe, offering affordable flights to and from the UK.

4. **Virgin Atlantic:** Known for long-haul international flights, Virgin Atlantic primarily operates flights between the UK and North America, the Caribbean, and other international destinations.

5. **Jet2:** A UK-based budget airline, Jet2 offers flights to popular European destinations and domestic routes within the UK.

The Cheapest Times to Fly to the UK

The cost of flights to the UK can fluctuate depending on several factors, including the time of year, demand, and how far in advance you book. To get the best deal, consider the following:

- **Travel During Off-Peak Seasons:**

  - **Winter (January to March)** – After the holiday season, flights tend to be cheaper. The months of January, February, and early March are generally less busy, with fewer tourists traveling to the UK.

  - **Autumn (September to November)** – Late September to early November is also an affordable time to fly, as it falls outside the peak summer travel period and major holidays.

- **Avoid Peak Travel Periods:**

  - **Summer (June to August)** – This is the busiest and most expensive season for flying to the UK, as many tourists visit the country for holidays. Prices for flights and accommodation can be much higher.

  - **Holidays (Christmas and Easter)** – During the Christmas (December) and Easter (April) holidays, flights tend to be more expensive due to increased demand.

- **Best Time to Book:** It's generally recommended to book at least six to eight weeks in advance to secure the best prices. Prices are often higher for last-minute bookings or when there are major events or holidays.

- **Midweek Flights:** Flying on Tuesdays, Wednesdays, or Thursdays tends to be cheaper than flying on weekends when demand is higher.

When to Visit?

The best time to visit the UK depends on what you're looking for— whether it's good weather, fewer crowds, or specific events. **Spring (April to June)** and **autumn (September to November)** offer mild weather, fewer tourists, and beautiful landscapes, with spring bringing blooming gardens and autumn offering colorful fall foliage. **Summer (June to August)** is the warmest, with longer days and vibrant festivals, but it's also the busiest time, particularly in cities like London and Edinburgh. **Winter (December to February)** is cold and wet, but it's ideal for experiencing festive Christmas markets and cozy pub visits.

For **activities, summer** is perfect for outdoor adventures and major festivals like **Glastonbury** and **Wimbledon**, while **spring** and **autumn** are great for sightseeing, exploring historic sites, and enjoying the countryside The UK's diverse events and seasonal beauty ensure there's something to enjoy year-round; notable cultural events include **Edinburgh Festival Fringe** (August), the **Notting Hill Carnival** (August), and **Burns Night** (January).

 ## Do I Need a Visa?

Whether you need a visa to visit the UK depends on your nationality and the purpose of your trip. If you're from a country with a visa exemption agreement with the UK, such as the **United States**, **Canada**, **Australia**, or **New Zealand**, you typically **won't need a visa** for short visits. This includes trips for tourism, business, or family visits, usually lasting **up to six months**. However, even if you don't require a visa, you'll still need to meet certain entry requirements, such as having a valid passport, proof of sufficient funds for your stay, and a return or onward travel ticket.

On the other hand, if you're from a country that does require a visa to enter the UK, like **India**, **China**, or **Nigeria**, you'll need to apply for a **Standard Visitor Visa**. This visa allows you to stay in the UK for **up to six months** for activities like tourism, attending business meetings, or receiving medical treatment.

Regardless of whether you need a visa or not, all visitors are expected to present a **valid passport, sufficient funds to cover their stay**, and proof of return or onward travel. To be sure of your specific requirements, it's always a good idea to check the UK government's official website or consult your nearest British embassy or consulate before making travel plans.

How to Get Around

Getting around the UK as a tourist is easy thanks to its efficient and varied transportation options. The **train system** is one of the best ways to travel between cities, with high-speed trains connecting London to places like Manchester and Edinburgh in just a few hours. For getting around within cities, especially in London, the **Tube** (underground) is fast and convenient, while the iconic **double-decker buses** offer a scenic and practical way to explore. For longer distances, **National Express** and **Megabus** provide affordable intercity coach services.

Taxis, including the famous **black cabs**, are widely available, offering door-to-door service in cities, while **ride-hailing apps** like **Uber** are also common in major urban areas. If you prefer flexibility and plan to explore more rural areas, renting a car might be ideal, though driving on the left side of the road and navigating some areas can be challenging. In many cities, **bike-sharing schemes** offer an easy and eco-friendly way to get around, while walking is perfect for exploring smaller towns or city centers like **Oxford** or **Bath**.

For those traveling longer distances within the UK, **domestic flights** can be convenient, though train travel is often a more scenic and efficient choice. With a wide range of transport options available, getting around the UK is both simple and enjoyable for tourists.

 ## Monetary Advice

When visiting the UK, it's important to be familiar with the country's monetary system and how to manage your finances during your stay. The **national currency** of the UK is the **British Pound (£)**, often symbolized as **GBP (Great British Pound)**. Coins come in denominations of 1p, 2p, 5p, 10p, 20p, 50p, £1, and £2, while notes are typically in £5, £10, £20, and £50. Exchange rates fluctuate, so it's a good idea to check the current rate before you travel. Currency exchange is available at banks, exchange bureau, and airports, though rates at the airport can be less favorable.

Credit cards are widely accepted across the UK, especially in larger cities. Most places, from restaurants and hotels to shops and attractions, accept **Visa** and **Mastercard**, and increasingly **American Express**. Contactless payments, through a card or smartphone, are also common and make transactions faster and more convenient. If you're planning to use a credit card, be aware that some cards may charge **foreign transaction fees**, so it's worth checking with your bank before you travel.

Regarding the use of **other currencies**, while the UK officially only accepts the **British Pound**, you may find some tourist-heavy areas, especially in London, where certain shops might accept **Euros**, but this is not common, and the exchange rate may not be favorable. It's generally better to use pounds or pay with a credit card.

Bargaining

In the UK, bargaining is **not a common practice**. Prices are usually fixed, particularly in stores, restaurants, and public services. However, there may be some flexibility in areas like markets, antique shops, or when booking services directly. In general, it's best to expect fixed pricing and only consider negotiation in specific, informal settings.

Tipping

Tipping in the UK is **not mandatory** but appreciated for good service. In **restaurants**, if a service charge of 10-12.5 percent is not included, a tip of around **10-15 percent** is common. In **bars**, it's usual to leave small change or round up the bill. For **taxis**, adding **5-10 percent** or rounding up is typical. For **hotel staff**, a couple of pounds for services like porters or housekeeping is a kind gesture. Tipping is largely discretionary, and it's mainly reserved for good service.

British Hospitality

The UK is known for its **warm, friendly,** but often somewhat **reserved** hospitality. British people are generally polite and respectful, and their hospitality is rooted in a strong sense of **tradition** and **good manners.** While the UK may not have the loud, over-the-top hospitality that some cultures embrace, British hosts are attentive, welcoming, and helpful in a more understated way.

British hospitality is usually expressed through **politeness** and **thoughtful gestures.** For instance, guests are often offered tea or coffee upon arrival, and meals are a big part of socializing, whether it's a casual get-together or a formal dinner. The British also value their **personal space**, so hospitality often involves a balance of being warm and welcoming while respecting boundaries. In formal settings, you might receive an invitation to a meal or an event with plenty of notice, and it's customary to respond with gratitude and punctuality.

When it comes to what's **polite** and **impolite**, British culture places a high value on **good manners** and **respectful behavior**. Saying "please" and "thank you" is essential in both casual and formal interactions. **Queueing** (standing in line) is a significant part of British etiquette, and cutting in line is considered highly impolite. **Public displays of emotion**, such as loud arguing or excessive praise, are generally frowned upon, as the British often favor a more understated approach in social settings. In British culture, it is considered disrespectful to ask overly personal questions unless you have established a closer relationship with someone, as the British tend to be more reserved about sharing personal details with strangers.

CUSTOMS

IN THIS CHAPTER

- Travelers Entering the United Kingdom
- Customs Entitlements and Monetary Restrictions
- Restricted and Prohibited Items
- Five Practical Tips to Know Before You Go

CUSTOMS

Travelers Entering the UK[2]

To enter the UK, you'll need to meet specific requirements and have the necessary documents. These may vary based on your nationality, the purpose of your visit, and whether you require a visa.

Required documents include:

1. **Passport:** A valid passport is required for all visitors to the UK, and it must be valid for at least six months beyond the date of your arrival.

2. **Visa (if applicable):** If you're from a country that requires a visa to enter the UK, you must apply for the appropriate visa (e.g., Standard Visitor Visa) before traveling. Citizens of many countries, such as the US, Canada, and EU countries, don't require a visa for short visits.

3. **Proof of Funds:** You may need to show evidence that you have sufficient funds to support yourself during your stay.

4. **Return/Onward Ticket:** It's essential to have a return or onward travel ticket to show that you plan to leave the UK at the end of your visit.

---

2   https://www.gov.uk/uk-border-control/before-you-leave-for-the-uk

5. **Health Insurance (if applicable):** If you're traveling for more than just tourism, or you're staying for a long period, travel insurance covering health and emergencies is highly recommended, though not mandatory for tourists.

Upon arrival, you'll go through passport control, where an immigration officer will check your documents and may ask about the purpose of your visit, your accommodation, and your return plans. Depending on your nationality, you might simply get your passport stamped or scanned. If you need a visa, you'll have to present the appropriate documents. Be aware that you may be asked to declare certain items at customs, like cash over £10,000 (approximately US$12,893) or goods subject to duty. The UK also conducts security checks, so expect thorough screening of your luggage.

 Before traveling, it's wise to check the UK government's official website for the latest updates on entry requirements and travel advisories at **https://www.gov.uk/ foreign-travel-advice/usa/entry-requirements.**

Customs Entitlements and Monetary Restrictions

When visiting the UK, there are certain customs entitlements and monetary restrictions that you should be aware of to comply with UK regulations and avoid any complications at customs.

- **Duty-Free Goods:** You are allowed to bring in certain goods duty-free as part of your personal allowance. For instance, you can bring in alcohol, tobacco, and gifts without paying tax or duties, provided you stay within the specified limits.

  - **Alcohol:** Up to 42 liters of beer (about 11 gallons), 18 liters of wine (about 4.75 gallons), or 1 liter of spirits (like whiskey or vodka) per person.

- **Tobacco:** You are entitled to bring in 200 cigarettes, 100 cigarillos, 50 cigars, or 250g of tobacco (about 8.8 ounces) duty-free.

- **Gifts:** You can bring gifts worth up to £390 (about US$520) if traveling by air or sea, or £270 (about US$350) if traveling by land.

- **Personal Items:** Personal items such as clothing, toiletries, and other items for personal use are generally not subject to customs duties, as long as they are not excessive in quantity and are for personal use only.

- **Currency:** When entering the UK, you can bring unlimited amounts of money, but if you're carrying £10,000 (approximately US$12,893), or its equivalent in other currencies, or more, you must declare it at customs. This includes cash, checks, money orders, and other negotiable instruments. Failure to declare amounts over this limit can result in the seizure of the money and penalties. For amounts under £10,000, there is no need to declare your cash.

 ## Restricted and Prohibited Items[3]

When entering the UK, there are several restricted and prohibited items that travelers must be aware of to comply with customs regulations. These items are either banned outright or require special documentation to be imported.

Restricted Items:

1. **Food and Plant Products:** Certain fresh produce, meat, dairy products, and plants are restricted to prevent the spread of diseases and

---

3   https://www.gov.uk/bringing-goods-into-uk-personal-use/
banned-and-restricted-goods

pests. Items from outside the EU often require a phytosanitary certificate or may be prohibited altogether.

2. **Medication:** Some medications that are available over the counter in other countries may be classified as controlled substances in the UK. If you need to bring medication, make sure it's for personal use and ideally, carry a doctor's prescription or a letter explaining its necessity.

3. **Endangered Species:** Items made from endangered species, such as ivory, certain animal skins, and exotic plants, are regulated under the CITES (Convention on International Trade in Endangered Species). You cannot bring these into the UK without proper permits.

4. **Weapons and Firearms:** Bringing in firearms, explosives, and other weapons is tightly controlled. You must have a firearm certificate or a license for certain items like rifles, guns, or even some types of knives.

Prohibited Items:

1. **Illegal Drugs:** Bringing any illegal drugs into the UK is a criminal offense and can result in severe penalties, including imprisonment. This includes substances like marijuana (unless prescribed for medicinal use) and other controlled narcotics.

2. **Counterfeit Goods:** Importing counterfeit goods, such as fake designer clothing, pirated electronics, or knockoff branded products, is illegal and could result in the confiscation of items and legal action.

3. **Offensive Weapons:** Knives, sharp objects, and other items that could be deemed offensive weapons (even if intended for personal use) are prohibited. Some items, like folding knives or certain tools, may be restricted depending on their design or size.

4. **Certain Fireworks and Explosives:** Fireworks and other explosive materials are highly regulated. While some may be brought into the country for personal use, others are banned completely due to safety concerns.

5. **Pornographic Material:** Extremely graphic or illegal pornography is prohibited in the UK, and possession or importation of such material can result in legal action.

It's important to check the UK government's customs website or speak with a travel advisor for the most up-to-date list of restricted and prohibited items. Always ensure that any items you bring with you meet the necessary requirements. Bringing restricted or prohibited items into the UK can result in serious consequences, including the seizure of items, fines, and delays in your travel. For more severe offenses, such as possessing illegal drugs, counterfeit goods, or weapons, you could face criminal charges, including arrest and imprisonment. In some cases, you may be denied entry to the UK or deported, with a potential ban on re-entry.

 For a more detailed and complete list of restricted and prohibited items, you can visit the UK official customs website at **https://www.gov.uk/bringing-goods-into-uk-personal-use/banned-and-restricted-goods**.

 # Five Practical Tips to Know Before You Go

These small cultural nuances can help you blend in more easily and show respect for British customs, making your experience more enjoyable and rewarding:

1. **Tipping** in the UK is generally **not mandatory**, but it's appreciated for good service. In restaurants, a tip of **10-15 percent** is common if service isn't included in the bill. For taxi drivers, rounding up the fare is typical, and small tips (around £1-£2, or approximately US$1.30 to $2.60) for hotel staff or baristas are appreciated. However, you won't be expected to tip in fast-food places or casual cafes.

2. The UK is a **cashless society** to a large extent. Many places now accept **contactless payments** via credit cards, debit cards, or

mobile apps like **Apple Pay** and **Google Pay**. Carrying a lot of cash is unnecessary, and using your card is often quicker and more convenient.

3. The British take their queues seriously. Always **stand in line** (queue) for services, whether at the bus stop, a coffee shop, or an attraction. Cutting in line is considered impolite and can draw unwanted attention.

4. Brits value their **personal space**, especially in public settings like buses, trains, or even queues. It's customary to maintain a **comfortable distance** between people, so avoid standing too close to others, even if the space seems available.

5. Pubs are a big part of British social life. When you visit a pub, it's common to **order your drink at the bar** rather than being served at your table. This gives you a chance to engage with the bartender and other locals, which is a culturally significant aspect of British hospitality.

CRIME IN THE UK

CHAPTER 3

CRIME IN THE UK

Overview

The UK is generally considered a **safe country** for both residents and visitors, especially in comparison to other countries. However, like any nation, it does experience various types of crime. The crime rate in the UK has been **declining over the past few years**, with a notable reduction in violent crimes such as **homicides** and **burglaries**, although certain areas, particularly in large cities, may see higher rates of specific crimes like **theft** and **anti-social behavior**. As of the latest data, the crime rate was reported at approximately 84 incidents per 1,000 people as of September 2024, reflecting a 4 percent decrease from the previous year.[4] Despite these variations, the UK maintains a relatively high level of personal safety compared to many countries across the globe, being ranked 34th on the Global Peace Index.

Crime in the UK can be influenced by a range of factors including **poverty, social inequality, substance abuse**, and **youth unemployment**. Urban areas, particularly those with higher levels of socio-economic disadvantage, tend to experience more crime. Additionally, gang activity, **drug trafficking**, and the increasing use of **cybercrime** have contributed to certain crime trends in recent years. Historically, crime in the UK has fluctuated, with notable increases in certain types of crime during times of economic hardship or social unrest. However, **overall crime**

---

4   https://crimerate.co.uk/

rates have been **decreasing** in the past decade, thanks to improved law enforcement strategies, better security systems, and public awareness campaigns. While violent crimes like murder and robbery have seen reductions, certain **types of fraud, cybercrimes**, and **hate crimes** have been on the rise, partly driven by the digital age and greater online interactions.

Crime Hotspots in the UK[5]

While the UK is generally considered a safe destination, certain areas, particularly in larger cities, are known to have higher crime rates. **London**, as the capital, sees a range of criminal activities across its boroughs. Areas like **Westminster, Camden**, and **Hackney** often experience **higher levels of crime**, including violent incidents like **knife crime** and **petty theft**, especially in tourist-heavy districts such as Oxford Street. Similarly, in **Manchester**, neighborhoods like **Hulme** and **Cheetham Hill** have historically struggled with crime, including **burglary, robbery**, and an uptick in **drug-related offenses.**

Birmingham, the UK's second-largest city, also has areas such as **Aston** and **Handsworth** where crime rates are notably higher, with issues like **gang violence** and **vehicle theft** more common. In Liverpool, neighborhoods like **Toxteth** and **Everton** see elevated rates of **violent crime** and **anti-social behavior**, despite the city's ongoing efforts to improve safety. **Glasgow**, once infamous for gang-related violence, still experiences **knife crime** and **drug offenses** in areas such as **Partick** and **Govan**. **Leeds** and **Sheffield** also have their crime hotspots, including districts like **Harehills** in Leeds and **Burngreave** in Sheffield, where crimes like **robbery** and **drug abuse** are more prevalent.

These hotspots are often linked to socio-economic challenges such as **poverty, unemployment**, and **social inequality**, which can contribute to higher crime rates. Additionally, areas with heavy foot traffic, especially around tourist attractions, tend to attract **petty crimes** like **pickpocketing**. While these areas may experience higher levels of criminal activity,

---

5   https://en.uhomes.com/blog/most-dangerous-cities-in-the-uk

the UK's overall crime rate has been decreasing in recent years, and the UK generally has **lower violent crime rates than the US**, particularly in terms of **homicides** and **gun-related offenses**, due to stricter **gun control laws**. While both countries face property crimes and gang violence, the US sees higher rates of armed robbery and vehicle theft, largely due to widespread firearm use. The UK also faces **terrorism** risks, but the US struggles more with mass shootings and right-wing extremism.[6]

Crime Statistics

In the UK, the most **common types of crime** are **theft, anti-social behavior, violent crime**, and **drug-related offenses. Theft** is particularly widespread, with **shoplifting** and **pickpocketing** being frequent in busy urban areas and tourist hotspots. **Knife crime** has become a rising concern, particularly in cities like London, though overall violent crime remains lower than in many other countries. **Drug offenses,** particularly related to **drug trafficking** and **gang violence**, are also prominent in certain urban areas.

Law enforcement in the UK is generally considered to be **effective** in tackling crime. Police forces are highly trained, and there's strong cooperation between agencies, which has contributed to relatively low crime rates compared to other nations. However, there have been isolated incidents of **corruption** or **misconduct** within certain police forces, but these are not widespread and are usually addressed. The professionalism and effectiveness of the UK police generally maintain public trust, which helps keep crime levels manageable.

For **visitors and tourists, petty crime** such as **pickpocketing** and **bag-snatching** are the most prevalent concerns, especially in crowded tourist areas or on public transportation in major cities like London, Edinburgh, and Manchester. **Street scams**, where tourists are targeted by fraudsters posing as charity collectors or offering "too-good-to-be-true" deals, are also common. While violent crime against tourists is

---

6   https://www.nationmaster.com/country-info/compare/United-Kingdom/
     United-States/Crime/table

rare, it's always advisable for travelers to remain vigilant, especially in unfamiliar areas, and secure their belongings to avoid becoming targets.

Quick Safety Tips

- Be cautious of **pickpockets** in busy places like **tourist spots, train stations**, and **shopping districts.**

- Keep valuables like phones, wallets, and passports in **secure, zipped pockets** or a **money belt.**

- Stick to well-lit streets and avoid walking alone in unfamiliar or **isolated areas** after dark.

- Be cautious of **street scams** (e.g., fake charity collectors or overly friendly strangers asking for money).

- Stick to official **taxis** or **ride-hailing apps** like **Uber**, especially late at night, instead of accepting rides from unlicensed cabs.

- Keep a close eye on your belongings while using buses, trains, and the Underground, as these can be hotspots for **theft.**

CRIMINAL LAW VIOLATIONS

CRIMINAL LAW VIOLATIONS

Marijuana and Other Drugs in the UK

In the UK, the relationship with **marijuana** (cannabis) has evolved over time, but it remains **strictly regulated** under **drug laws**. Historically, cannabis was used for a variety of purposes, including medicinal and industrial (such as hemp for textiles), but it became illegal in the twentieth century under international drug treaties. The UK classifies cannabis as a **Class B drug**, which means **possession, production,** or **supply** is a **criminal offense**, carrying penalties ranging from fines and warnings to prison sentences.

In recent years, the UK has made distinctions between **medical** and **recreational** cannabis use. **Medical cannabis** was **legalized in 2018** for certain conditions, such as severe epilepsy, multiple sclerosis, and chronic pain, but access is tightly controlled. Patients need a prescription from a specialist doctor, and the use of medical marijuana is limited to specific formulations, like oils or capsules, rather than the traditional plant form. **Recreational cannabis**, however, remains **illegal** in the UK. Possession can lead to a warning, a fine, or **up to five years in prison**, while trafficking and production can result in much harsher penalties.[7]

Another growing concern in the UK is the rise of **synthetic cannabinoids**. These are man-made substances designed to mimic the effects

---

7   https://www.leafie.co.uk/articles/will-the-uk-legalise-cannabis

of cannabis but are often much stronger and more dangerous. They are sold under names like **"Spice"** or **"Black Mamba,"** and are typically found in the form of dried leaves sprayed with chemicals. These drugs are highly **unpredictable** and have been linked to numerous health issues, including severe psychiatric symptoms, increased risk of overdose, and even death. Despite being **banned** in the UK since 2016, synthetic cannabinoids remain an ongoing public health issue, especially in **prison populations** and among the homeless.

Laws Concerning Other Drugs[8]

The UK has strict laws regarding all **controlled substances**, which are divided into three categories under the **Misuse of Drugs Act:**

- **Class A drugs**, including **heroin, cocaine, ecstasy, LSD**, and **methamphetamines**, are considered the most dangerous and carry the severest penalties. Possession of a Class A drug can result in up to seven years in prison, while trafficking can lead to **life imprisonment**.

- **Class B drugs**, like **cannabis, amphetamine, barbiturates**, and **synthetic cannabinoids**, come with somewhat lesser penalties. Possession can lead to up to **five years in prison** and trafficking up to **14 years.**

- **Class C drugs**, including substances like **benzodiazepines** (such as **Valium**) and **anabolic steroids**, have **lesser penalties**, but possession can still result in up to **two years in prison.**

Additionally, the **Psychoactive Substances Act 2016** bans the production, supply, or possession of **psychoactive substances** (often marketed as "legal highs") that can alter mood or perception. These include synthetic cannabinoids (like **Spice**) and other substances that mimic the effects of illegal drugs. Violation of this law can result in up to **seven years in prison.**

Enforcement of drug laws varies across the UK. Police forces may issue **warnings** for small quantities of cannabis, particularly for first-time

---

8   https://www.gov.uk/penalties-drug-possession-dealing

offenders, but continue to crack down on larger-scale distribution and trafficking. **Public opinion** on drug laws has been shifting in recent years, with growing support for **decriminalizing** cannabis or making it **legal for recreational use**, similar to other countries like Canada and certain US states. However, the UK government maintains a firm stance against recreational use and has resisted calls for broader reform.

Prescription Medication

When traveling to the UK with prescription medication, it's essential to be aware of the rules and regulations to avoid any complications at customs. The UK has strict laws concerning the **importation of medication**, whether it's prescribed or bought over the counter.

If you are bringing **prescription medication**, you should carry a **copy of the prescription** along with a **doctor's letter** that explains the purpose of the medication. This will help demonstrate that the medication is for personal use. It's also important to ensure that the medication is **legal in the UK**, as some drugs that are commonly prescribed in other countries may be classified as controlled substances in the UK. For example, certain painkillers, **benzodiazepines**, or **stimulants** are considered **controlled drugs**. If your medication falls into this category, it's advisable to notify UK authorities before your trip. In some cases, you may need to apply for a **Personal Import License** to bring the medication into the country.

For **over-the-counter medications**, most common remedies, such as **pain relievers** or **cold treatments**, can generally be brought into the UK without issue. However, you should still check the ingredients to ensure the medication does not contain restricted substances. For instance, some **decongestants** containing **pseudoephedrine** are regulated, as they can be used in the illegal production of drugs.

Failing to follow these regulations can lead to serious consequences. If you arrive at the border with **unapproved medication** or **controlled substances** without proper documentation, authorities may **seize the medication**, and you could face **fines** or even **criminal charges** in extreme cases. To avoid such issues, it's always a good idea to **research** your medication before traveling and, if necessary, consult UK authorities or your healthcare provider. Being prepared ensures that your trip remains smooth and free from unnecessary complications.

General Questions

1. *Is cannabis legal in the UK?* **No**. Cannabis is **illegal for recreational use** in the UK. However, **medical cannabis** was **legalized in 2018** for certain conditions, but it is strictly regulated and only available through a specialist prescription.

2. *Where can I legally purchase marijuana in the UK?* Cannabis cannot be legally purchased for recreational use in the UK. It is available only through a prescription for medical purposes, and only for specific conditions. These medical cannabis products (e.g., oils or capsules) can be prescribed by a specialist doctor but not bought over the counter or in shops.

3. *Can I have marijuana on my person or in my hotel room in the UK?* **No**. It is illegal to have marijuana on your person or in a hotel room in the UK. Possession of cannabis is a criminal offense, and carrying it, whether on your person or in your accommodation, can lead to legal penalties. Even if you're staying in a private hotel room, possession is still prohibited unless you have a legal prescription for medical cannabis.

4. *Are there any other exceptions to the possession and consumption of cannabis in the UK?* **Yes**. The only exception to cannabis possession and consumption in the UK is for medical use. Since 2018, medical cannabis has been legal for patients with specific conditions, such as severe epilepsy or chronic pain, but only with a prescription from a specialist doctor.

5. ***What are the penalties for possessing and consuming other types of illicit drugs in the UK?*** In the UK, penalties for drug possession vary by classification. Class A drugs (e.g., heroin, cocaine) can lead to up to seven years in prison for possession and life imprisonment for trafficking. Class B drugs (e.g., cannabis, amphetamine) carry up to five years for possession and 14 years for trafficking. Class C drugs (e.g., steroids) carry up to two years for possession. First-time offenders may receive warnings or fines for Class B drugs, but drug-related offenses can lead to arrest and prosecution, especially for drug driving (driving while under the influence of drugs).

 **Law of the Land Hypothetical**

HYPOTHETICAL: *Sarah is a tourist visiting the UK from Canada. She has a prescription for medical cannabis in her home country to help manage chronic pain. Before her trip, she ensures her medication is in its original packaging with the prescription label. Upon arrival at Heathrow Airport, customs officers ask to search her bag and find her cannabis medication.*

Can Sarah legally bring her medical cannabis into the UK, and what steps should she have taken before traveling?

ANSWER: *No. Sarah cannot legally bring her cannabis medication into the UK without taking extra steps. While medical cannabis is legal in the UK for certain conditions, **the prescription must be issued by a UK specialist doctor**. To legally bring her medication, Sarah would need to apply for a Personal Import License from the UK Home Office before traveling. Without this, her cannabis would be considered illegal, and customs may seize it, possibly leading to fines or legal action.*

 **Takeaways**

- Medical cannabis is legal for specific conditions, but recreational cannabis remains illegal, with penalties ranging from fines to five years in prison for possession.

- Medical cannabis requires a specialist prescription and is only available in specific forms like oils or capsules. Foreign prescriptions aren't automatically valid.

- The UK has banned the production, supply, and possession of psychoactive substances, including synthetic cannabinoids. Violations can result in up to seven years in prison.

- Travelers must ensure their prescription medications are legal in the UK. Some may require a Personal Import License to avoid legal issues.

- While police may issue warnings for small amounts of cannabis, larger-scale trafficking and distribution are heavily prosecuted. Public opinion on drug laws is shifting, but the UK government remains firm against recreational use.

CHAPTER 5

ALCOHOL-RELATED OFFENSES

IN THIS CHAPTER

- Alcohol-Related Offenses
- Alcohol Regulation
- Things to Remember
- General Questions
- Law of the Land Hypothetical
- Takeaways

CHAPTER 5

ALCOHOL-RELATED OFFENSES

Alcohol-Related Offenses

Alcohol has long been a central part of life in the UK, deeply embedded in both its social fabric and cultural identity. From ancient times, the British brewed **ale** and **mead**, with monasteries refining brewing methods in the medieval period. Ale became a staple of daily life, safer than water and more nourishing. As time passed, drinking beer and wine evolved into a **social ritual**, with the **pub** emerging as a **key social institution** by the sixteenth century.

The eighteenth century brought a darker side, with the "Gin Craze" flooding London's streets, leading to public disorder. Efforts to curb drinking were met with resistance, but alcohol remained an essential part of British culture.[9] The two World Wars further cemented alcohol's role, offering a means of coping with hardship and a place for people to connect and celebrate.

In the twentieth century, the **rise of the British pub** became iconic, and the act of "going to the pub" became a deeply ingrained social practice. Yet, concerns over alcohol's health effects grew, leading to public health campaigns and more moderate drinking habits.[10] In recent

---

9   https://www.adph.org.uk/resources/the-history-of-alcohol/

10 https://rehabsuk.com/blog/
    cheers-or-concerns-navigating-the-drinking-culture-in-the-uk/

years, younger generations have embraced alcohol-free alternatives and the "sober curious" movement, marking a shift toward more mindful drinking.

Despite these changes, alcohol remains a key part of British life. The pub still serves as a space for connection, and drinking continues to play a role in socializing, celebrations, and even identity. The relationship with alcohol in the UK is evolving, but its influence remains significant in everyday life.

In England, several alcoholic drinks are considered quintessentially English, deeply rooted in the country's culture and history. **Ale**, particularly **cask ale**, is central to traditional pub culture, with **bitters** and **pale ales** being common varieties. **Pimm's**, a gin-based cocktail mixed with fruit and mint, is a popular summer drink, especially at events like Wimbledon.

Gin is another iconic English drink, particularly **London Dry Gin**, often served in a **Gin and Tonic**. English gin has enjoyed a revival, with craft distilleries offering a variety of flavors. **English wine**, especially sparkling wines from regions like Sussex and Kent, has gained recognition, rivaling Champagne.

Cider, particularly from regions like Somerset, is a refreshing, traditional English drink enjoyed in pubs, especially in the summer. Lastly, **English whisky**, though less famous than Scottish varieties, has seen a resurgence in recent years, with distilleries producing single malts and blended whiskies. These drinks reflect England's rich and evolving drinking culture. Though non-alcoholic, **tea** remains a cherished British tradition, with **afternoon tea** standing as a symbol of British culture and comfort. These drinks illustrate the UK's diverse and evolving drinking habits, from traditional ales to modern gins and local wines, highlighting the nation's complex relationship with alcohol.

Alcohol Regulation

Alcohol consumption in the UK is regulated by several pieces of legislation, with the primary ones being the **Licensing Act 2003** and the **Alcohol (Minimum Pricing) (Scotland) Act 2012**. The Licensing Act sets out the rules for the sale and supply of alcohol in England and Wales, including the licensing of premises and the provision of alcohol. This law aims to prevent alcohol-related crime and disorder, protect children from harm, and promote public safety. In Scotland, **minimum unit pricing** was introduced in 2018, setting a minimum price for alcohol per unit of 50p (about US$0.65), aimed at reducing excessive drinking, particularly among those who buy cheap, high-strength alcohol. Northern Ireland also has similar licensing laws that govern alcohol sales, but the specifics may vary.

Additionally, **alcohol advertising** in the UK is **strictly regulated**. Alcohol advertising in the UK is tightly regulated to prevent targeting children, promoting excessive drinking, or suggesting alcohol is necessary for social success. Ads must adhere to the Broadcasting Code and ASA rules and are banned in environments like children's programming or websites aimed at young audiences. Brands sponsoring events must also ensure their logos are not visible in places where children are likely to be present.

Alcohol regulations in the UK are enforced by local authorities, the police, and other government bodies. The enforcement of the **Licensing Act 2003** involves local councils that issue and review alcohol licenses for pubs, clubs, and stores. Violations, such as selling alcohol without a license or selling to minors, can lead to fines, the suspension of licenses, or even imprisonment. In the case of underage sales, shopkeepers or pub owners can face fines and lose their license to sell alcohol. For breaches related to alcohol advertising, the **ASA** (Advertising Standards Authority) plays a key role. The ASA investigates complaints and can force advertisers to withdraw or amend ads that breach the rules. Further penalties can include fines for advertisers that do not comply. In Scotland, the **minimum unit pricing** law is enforced by local authorities and police. Sellers found violating this law by selling alcohol below the minimum price can face fines or have their alcohol license revoked.

The legal drinking age in the UK varies slightly across the nations, but in general:

- **England, Wales, and Northern Ireland:** The legal age for purchasing alcohol is **18**. However, those 16 or 17 may consume beer, wine, or cider in a pub or restaurant when accompanied by an adult.
- **Scotland:** The legal age for purchasing alcohol is also **18**, though like elsewhere, 16- or 17-year-olds may consume alcohol with a meal at a licensed establishment when accompanied by an adult.

There are strict penalties for selling alcohol to those underage. Shops and licensed premises can be fined or have their licenses revoked if they are caught selling to minors. Additionally, underage drinking in public places can result in penalties for the individuals involved, including fines or being escorted home by the police.

 ## Things to Remember

- **Drinking Age:** The legal drinking age for purchasing alcohol in the UK is **18**.
- **ID:** You may be asked to show a valid ID if you appear under 25 to purchase alcohol. Acceptable forms of ID include a passport, driving license, or PASS card.
- **Public Consumption:** Drinking alcohol in public is generally legal, but local councils can impose restrictions in certain areas or events. Consumption in designated alcohol-free zones or specific public places may be prohibited.
- **Public Drunkenness:** While public drunkenness itself is not illegal, causing disruption or being disorderly in public can lead to fines, arrest, or imprisonment for offenses like "drunk and disorderly behavior."
- **Drunk Driving:** The legal blood alcohol concentration (**BAC**) limit is **0.08 percent** in England, Wales, and Northern Ireland, and **0.05 percent** in Scotland. Penalties for exceeding the limit

include fines, driving bans, and imprisonment, especially if the driver is involved in an accident.

- **Purchase of Alcohol:** Alcohol can be purchased at licensed premises such as pubs, shops, and supermarkets between 6 a.m. and 11 p.m., although local regulations may vary. Only individuals over the age of 18 can legally purchase alcohol.

- **Alcohol Permits:** For private events where alcohol is sold, a Temporary Event Notice (TEN) is required. No special permits are needed for private, non-commercial gatherings where alcohol is consumed but not sold.

- **Illegal Alcohol:** The sale of counterfeit or unlicensed alcohol is a concern, particularly when it comes to illicit imports or home-made alcohol. Selling or possessing illegal alcohol can result in heavy fines and imprisonment.

 **General Questions**

1. *Can I possess an open container in public?* **Yes**. In the UK, possessing an open container of alcohol in public is generally **legal**, but local councils can impose restrictions in certain areas, such as **Alcohol Control Zones**. In these areas, drinking alcohol in public may be prohibited, and violators could face fines or be asked to dispose of the alcohol. Outside these zones, it's typically allowed to carry and consume alcohol in public.

2. *Can I drink alcohol on public transport in the UK?* Drinking alcohol on public transport in the UK depends on the provider and location. While it's allowed on most trains, buses and the London Underground have specific bans. Always check with the specific transport provider for their alcohol policy and be aware that disruptive behavior related to drinking can lead to fines or removal from the transport.

Law of the Land Hypothetical

QUESTION: Lucy, 22, attends a music festival in the UK where alcohol is being sold. She buys a can of beer and proceeds to drink it while watching a performance in the festival's outdoor area. A security guard approaches her and asks her to pour the beer out, citing the festival's rules against drinking alcohol in certain public spaces. Was the security guard within his rights to ask Lucy to pour out her beer?

ANSWER: *Yes. The security guard was within his rights. While it is legal to drink alcohol in public spaces in the UK, event organizers, including at festivals, can set their own rules regarding alcohol consumption. If the festival has specific areas where drinking is not permitted or has restrictions in place for safety or crowd control, the security guard can enforce those rules. Lucy should comply with the event's regulations, and refusing to do so could lead to removal from the event.*

Takeaways

- Alcohol has been a part of British culture for centuries, from ancient ales to modern gins and ciders. The pub remains a central social hub, even as drinking habits shift toward more mindful consumption, especially among younger generations.

- UK alcohol laws, such as the Licensing Act 2003 and minimum unit pricing in Scotland, regulate the sale, advertising, and consumption of alcohol to promote public health and safety. Advertising is tightly controlled to prevent targeting minors or encouraging excessive drinking.

- Local authorities and police enforce alcohol laws, with penalties like fines, license revocation, or imprisonment for violations such as selling to minors or improper advertising.

- The legal age to purchase alcohol is 18, though 16- and 17-year-olds can drink with a meal at a pub when accompanied by an adult. Sellers must request ID from anyone who looks under 25.

- Drinking alcohol in public is usually allowed, but local restrictions may apply. The legal blood alcohol concentration (BAC) limit is 0.08 percent in most areas, with penalties including fines, bans, and imprisonment for those exceeding the limit, especially after accidents.

FIREARM & AMMUNITION OFFENSES

CHAPTER 6

FIREARM & AMMUNITION OFFENSES

Current Firearm Status[11]

The United Kingdom has some of the most stringent firearm laws in the world. In response to numerous gun violence events, ownership of firearms is **highly regulated**. To legally own a firearm, individuals must meet strict criteria. Generally, applicants must be over 18, have a clean criminal record, and be deemed fit to possess a firearm by local authorities. For certain types of firearms, like handguns, ownership is severely restricted and only permitted under specific circumstances, such as for professional sportsmen or those with a genuine need (e.g., farmers). Additionally, prospective gun owners must pass **comprehensive background checks** and show a **valid reason for possessing a firearm**, such as for hunting, shooting sports, or agricultural work. Firearm licenses are issued by local police forces, and applicants must provide secure storage for the weapon.

The UK also has strict rules on the types of firearms that can be legally owned. The main categories include:

---

11 https://www.standard.co.uk/news/uk/uk-ban-hand-guns-laws-rules-ownership-b1070718.html

- **Shotguns:** Shotguns are the most common firearms legally owned by the public. They are typically used for sporting purposes, such as clay pigeon shooting or hunting. Owners need a **Shotgun Certificate** (SGC) to possess them, and there are limits on the number of rounds a shotgun can hold.

- **Rifles:** Rifles, typically used for hunting or target shooting, can also be legally owned under a **Firearm Certificate** (FAC). The owner must provide a valid reason for owning a rifle, such as shooting sports or pest control. There are limits on ammunition and the number of rifles an individual can own.

- **Air guns:** Air guns with a muzzle energy of over 12 ft-lbs (foot-pounds) are classified as firearms in the UK and also require a **Firearm Certificate**, while those with lower energy levels are less regulated but still require age verification for purchase.

- **Handguns:** Handguns are largely banned in the UK following the **1997 Firearms (Amendment) Act** after the Dunblane Massacre, with exceptions for certain professionals (e.g., Olympic shooters) under tightly controlled circumstances.

Overall, gun ownership in the UK is allowed under very specific, regulated circumstances, and possession limits are strictly enforced. Each firearm owner is subject to regular police checks, and weapons must be securely stored to prevent misuse.

Legal Requirements for Purchasing, Carrying, and Using a Firearm

The legal landscape for purchasing, carrying, and using firearms in the United Kingdom is inherently designed to **prioritize public safety**. The requirement for obtaining certificates, conducting background checks, demonstrating good reasons for ownership, and adhering to regulations, as discussed above, ensures that firearm ownership is limited to responsible individuals who contribute positively to society.

In the UK, **carrying a firearm in public is strictly prohibited** unless the individual has a special license for specific activities such as shooting competitions or professional duties like those of gamekeepers or farmers. For recreational shooting, firearms must always be transported in a secure, unloaded state to and from licensed shooting ranges or hunting grounds. Carrying a firearm in public without a legitimate reason is illegal and can result in **severe penalties.**

When **transporting firearms,** they must be stored in **a locked case**, and ammunition should be carried separately to reduce the risk of accidents. It's essential that firearms are not easily accessible during transit to ensure safety and prevent misuse.

Firearms are permitted only for approved activities (e.g., hunting, target shooting etc.), and **personal defense** is **not a valid reason for firearm possession** or use in the UK. When using firearms for target shooting, individuals must do so at **licensed ranges** that adhere to strict safety and legal regulations. Likewise, when hunting or engaging in pest control, users must follow legal guidelines on where and when it's permissible to hunt, as well as which animals are legal to hunt. Any deviation from these regulations, such as hunting without a license or targeting protected species, is illegal.

Firearm owners and users must demonstrate responsible behavior at all times. **Reckless or negligent use of a firearm can lead to serious criminal charges**, including manslaughter or reckless endangerment, if it results in harm or danger to others. Violating firearm laws, carrying a firearm without a license, or misusing a weapon can lead to severe penalties, including **imprisonment, fines, and the revocation of firearm licenses.** Serious offenses, such as possessing illegal firearms or using a firearm in the commission of a crime, may result in **lengthy prison sentences.**

Firearm Restrictions for Visitors[12]

Traveling to the UK with firearms involves navigating a complex framework of legal regulations that prioritize public safety. Visitors intending

---

12   https://www.gov.uk/guidance/import-controls-on-offensive-weapons

to bring firearms must first obtain a **Visitor's Firearm Permit** or a **Visitor's Shotgun Permit**, depending on the type of firearm. The application for these permits must be sponsored by a UK-based individual or organization with the necessary firearms certificate. This process is thorough, requiring applicants to provide detailed information about the firearms they wish to bring, including serial numbers, along with proof that they hold equivalent permits in their home country. It is advisable for visitors to apply for these permits well in advance of their travel dates, as processing can take several weeks.

Additionally, the UK imposes strict restrictions on certain firearms, notably prohibiting most handguns and semi-automatic weapons unless specifically authorized for events like the Olympics. Visitors are also limited in the amount of ammunition they can bring, closely regulated based on the firearms in their possession. Upon entry, it is essential for visitors to declare their firearms at customs and carry all relevant documentation to avoid complications. These regulations ensure that firearm ownership remains safe and responsible, allowing visitors to engage in intended activities while complying with UK law.

 **Penalties**[13]

Possession of Illegal Firearms

It is illegal to possess a firearm without the proper license. This includes firearms that are not registered or are prohibited.

Penalties:

- **Maximum sentence:** Life imprisonment.

---

13 https://www.sentencingcouncil.org.uk/sentencing-and-the-council/about-sentencing-guidelines/about-published-guidelines/firearms-offences/)

- **Minimum sentence:** 5 years imprisonment for possession of prohibited firearms or ammunition.

This applies to both residents and visitors. If a visitor brings an illegal firearm into the country, they will be subject to these penalties.

Trafficking and Smuggling Firearms

Firearms trafficking or smuggling involves the illegal movement or distribution of firearms within the UK or across international borders.

Penalties:

- **Maximum sentence:** Life imprisonment.
- **Minimum sentence:** 7 years imprisonment.

The scale of trafficking, involvement of organized crime, and the type of firearms involved (e.g., automatic weapons) can lead to heavier penalties.

Firearm Use in Crimes:

The use of a firearm in the commission of a crime, such as armed robbery, assault, or murder, is heavily penalized.

Penalties:

- **Maximum sentence:** Life imprisonment for violent crimes involving firearms (e.g., murder, attempted murder).
- **Other crimes:** Sentences can vary depending on the specific crime (e.g., armed robbery can carry a sentence of up to life imprisonment).

Using firearms to intimidate, cause harm, or with intent to kill will result in more severe penalties.

Unauthorized Carrying of Firearms

It is illegal to carry a firearm in public without a valid firearm or shotgun certificate, or where there is no legitimate reason for carrying the weapon (e.g., hunting, sport shooting).

Penalties:

- **Maximum sentence:** Up to 5 years imprisonment for unauthorized carrying.

- **Fine:** A fine may also be imposed in addition to imprisonment, depending on the severity of the offense.

Even if the firearm is legally owned, carrying it without the necessary permits or outside the scope of lawful use (e.g., for personal defense) is a criminal offense.

 **General Questions**

1. *What happens if the police catch me carrying a firearm in the UK?* If the police catch you carrying a firearm in the UK without proper authorization, the situation will quickly turn serious. First, you'll likely be arrested on suspicion of illegal possession. The police will seize the firearm, and you could face charges for carrying a weapon without the necessary license or certificate. Depending on the circumstances, such as whether the firearm is prohibited or used in a crime, you could be looking at a prison sentence of up to **five years**, or in extreme cases, even **life imprisonment.** A conviction would also result in a permanent criminal

record, severely impacting your future, from employment prospects to international travel. The UK has zero tolerance for illegal firearm possession, and the penalties reflect the importance of maintaining public safety.

2. *Can travelers bring ammunition into the UK for shooting sports or hunting?* **Yes**. Travelers can bring ammunition into the UK for shooting sports or hunting, but only with **prior approval** and **strict conditions**. You must apply for a **firearm or shotgun certificate** in advance, declare the ammunition upon arrival, and ensure that it complies with UK regulations. Without the necessary permits, bringing ammunition into the UK is illegal and could result in arrest, fines, or imprisonment.

 ## Law of the Land True Story[14]

On October 26, 2023, a man was sentenced to five years in prison for attempting to purchase a Glock 17 handgun and 100 rounds of ammunition from the dark web. The individual paid £1,000 (approximately US$1,289) in cryptocurrency for the weapon, which was intercepted by US law enforcement before it could be shipped. During an investigation, authorities uncovered disturbing internet searches on the man's laptop, including terms like "primary school in Glasgow," "Dunblane school massacre," and "when do schools break up for Christmas 2022." These searches raised concerns about a potential school attack, adding to the ongoing terrorism threat in the UK.

This incident is part of a broader trend of increasing concerns about firearm-related terrorist attacks in the UK. Recent cases highlight the intent of terrorist actors to use firearms in attacks, with disrupted plots linked to both extreme right-wing and Islamist groups. Despite the stringent UK firearm laws and proactive counterterrorism measures,

---

14   https://www.poolre.co.uk/terrorism-threat-publications/man-sentenced-for-buying-gun-and-making-online-searches-about-school-shootings/

such threats remain persistent, particularly targeting locations with high foot traffic, such as schools. This case underscores the evolving nature of the threat, especially in the context of young people potentially becoming radicalized and plotting attacks.

Takeaways

- The UK has stringent firearm regulations, with ownership allowed only for specific purposes like hunting or sport shooting. Handguns are heavily restricted.

- To purchase or carry a firearm, individuals must obtain the necessary licenses, undergo background checks, and demonstrate a valid need for ownership.

- Visitors must apply for a special firearm permit to bring guns into the UK, with strict limits on ammunition and required sponsorship from a UK-based individual.

- Violating firearm laws can result in severe penalties, including life imprisonment for possession of illegal firearms, trafficking, or using guns in crimes.

- UK laws prioritize safety, with strict rules on firearm use, transport, and storage to prevent misuse and criminal activity.

PROSTITUTION

CHAPTER 7

PROSTITUTION

Overview

In the UK, prostitution itself is **legal**, but related activities such as **brothel-keeping**, **pimping**, and **soliciting in public** are **criminal offenses**. The legal framework focuses on preventing exploitation, particularly human trafficking and coercion, by criminalizing the exploitation of sex workers. Some areas have experimented with **decriminalizing street prostitution** and creating **safe zones** to improve worker safety and reduce harm.

The root causes of prostitution are linked to **poverty, homelessness, gender inequality**, and **trafficking**. Many people turn to sex work due to **financial hardship** or **lack of opportunities**, often compounded by **substance abuse** or **mental health** struggles. Regulatory trends are increasingly focusing on **harm reduction** and **decriminalization**. Some advocate for a **New Zealand-style approach**, where sex work is decriminalized to improve workers' safety, health, and legal rights. Public campaigns aim to reduce demand for sex work, while authorities continue to tackle exploitation and abuse in the sex trade, striving to balance worker protection with public safety.

Laws and Penalties[15]

Prostitution itself is legal in the UK. However, certain activities surrounding it are criminalized to reduce exploitation, abuse, and public safety risks. Key regulations and corresponding penalties include:

- **Brothel-Keeping:** Up to 7 years imprisonment.
- **Living Off the Earnings of Prostitution (Pimping or Trafficking):** Up to 14 years imprisonment.
- **Soliciting in Public (Street-Based Prostitution):** Fines or up to 6 months imprisonment for repeat offenders.
- **Paying for Sex with Someone Who is Controlled or Exploited (Coercion or Trafficking):** Up to 7 years imprisonment.
- **Human Trafficking for Prostitution:** Up to 14 years imprisonment, with the possibility of life imprisonment for severe cases of exploitation.

The legal framework governing sex work in the UK presents a set of requirements that sex workers must navigate in their efforts to operate safely and legally. As society evolves and discussions surrounding sex work continue, it is imperative that law enforcement practices and legislation reflect a balanced and humane approach to the complexities of sex work, recognizing the need for safety, health support, and legal protections for those involved in this often-stigmatized profession.

Prostitution Practices

Reliable statistics on prostitution in the UK are often hard to come by due to the illegal nature of many associated activities, such as street solicitation and brothel-keeping. However, some key data and studies provide insight into the prevalence and nature of sex work.

---

15   https://www.politics.co.uk/reference/prostitution/

According to the National Crime Agency (NCA), there are estimated to be around **80,000 sex workers** in the UK. This figure includes a mix of street-based and indoor workers, as well as those working through escort agencies or online platforms. Research suggests that **street-based prostitution** is in decline, with estimates showing fewer than 2,000 women involved in street-based sex work in some areas. This decline is partly due to the increased shift toward indoor work and online platforms. Nevertheless, street prostitution still remains prevalent in some cities like London, Manchester, and Glasgow. Local authorities and police regularly patrol these areas and may issue fines or warnings to individuals involved in street prostitution.

While precise numbers are difficult to obtain, studies indicate that **indoor prostitution**, which includes brothels and escort services, is more common. **Brothels**, although illegal, still operate under the radar, with the UK Home Office acknowledging their existence but focusing on dismantling trafficking networks linked to these establishments. Brothels can vary in size, from small apartments to large businesses. While brothels are illegal, "indoor workers" often use them, sometimes with third-party operators managing or controlling the environment. In some cases, brothels can also involve trafficking victims or exploited workers. Additionally, independent and agency-based **escorts** make up a significant proportion of the sex work industry in the UK. These individuals are often self-employed and advertise their services through online platforms, magazines, or word of mouth. Some may work from their own homes, while others may be booked for outcalls (visiting clients at their hotels or residences). While escorting is legal, many of these workers still face risks related to safety and exploitation.

The rise of the **internet** has significantly changed the landscape of prostitution. **Online escort services** have become one of the most common forms of sex work. **Independent escorts** advertise their services through websites, social media, or platforms like AdultWork.com. The Home Office estimates that over **50 percent of sex work** in the UK now takes place online. In some cases, **massage parlors** operate as fronts for prostitution. These establishments may provide legitimate massage services while also offering sexual services in a more discreet environment. The line between legal and illegal services in these businesses can often be blurred.

Many local authorities, particularly in larger cities, have adopted a **harm-reduction approach** to address prostitution. In cities where street prostitution remains prevalent, local authorities may engage in **crackdowns** on street solicitation. Areas with high levels of street sex work may experience increased police activity, with some cities employing **"managed zones"** that regulate where sex workers can operate, ensuring they do so safely while reducing the impact on local residents. In contrast, some regions have a **zero-tolerance approach** to street prostitution. For instance, in parts of Manchester and Bristol, local authorities have actively sought to clear areas of street-based sex work, with increased police presence and the issuance of fines. These areas are often subject to stricter policing measures.

While some local authorities prioritize enforcement, **advocacy groups** like **UKNSWP (UK Network of Sex Work Projects)** and **SWARM (Sex Workers' Advocacy and Resistance Movement)** actively challenge policies they see as harmful to sex workers. These groups push for **decriminalization** and **better working conditions** for sex workers, arguing that the current system criminalizes vulnerable individuals, pushes sex work underground, and increases the risks they face.

Sex Trafficking and Exploitation

Sex trafficking and exploitation are **significant concerns** in the UK, as the country has been a destination and transit point for trafficking victims. This issue is tied to global criminal networks that exploit vulnerable individuals, often through coercion, manipulation, or force. Victims, including both adults and minors, may be trafficked for sex work, and they often experience severe abuse and lack of freedom.

The UK's **high demand for sex services**, particularly in cities with large populations or high tourist activity, makes it a target for traffickers. Additionally, **economic inequality**, **lack of social support**, and **personal vulnerabilities**, such as homelessness or immigration status, can make people more susceptible to exploitation.

Certain areas of the UK are more vulnerable to sex trafficking due to factors like economic disparity, high levels of organized crime, and heavy tourism. Major cities like **London, Manchester**, and **Birmingham**, as well as **ports** and **transportation hubs**, tend to be focal points for trafficking activities. Some regions with higher concentrations of sex work or illegal brothels may also be hotspots for exploitation. Authorities are continually working to combat trafficking, but it remains a significant challenge due to the hidden nature of the crime and the complexity of international trafficking networks.

The demographic most at risk of sex trafficking in the UK includes vulnerable individuals, particularly **young people** (16-24), **migrants**, the **homeless**, and **people in poverty**. Women, especially from disadvantaged backgrounds, are often targeted, though men and transgender individuals can also be victims. Minors, particularly those in care or with abuse histories, are highly vulnerable.

The UK government has taken steps to combat sex trafficking through the **Modern Slavery Act 2015**, which aims to protect victims and target traffickers. The National Crime Agency (NCA) and non-government organizations like ECPAT UK work to dismantle trafficking networks and support victims. Despite these efforts, challenges remain due to the hidden nature of trafficking and the complexity of international smuggling routes.

 ## Sex Tourism and Public Health

While the UK is **not typically renowned** as a leading destination for sex tourism on the scale of countries such as Thailand or the Dominican Republic, sex tourism is nonetheless present. Certain areas, particularly major cities like London, Manchester, and Birmingham, attract individuals seeking sex services, including those from abroad. These locations often have a combination of street-based sex work, brothels, escort services, and online platforms catering to both domestic and international clients.

While the UK **doesn't have specific tourist destinations solely dedicated to sex tourism**, its reputation as a major global hub for business, tourism, and events means that some tourists may seek sex services during their visit. The services are often advertised through online platforms, escort agencies, or discreet advertisements in certain local establishments. Websites like AdultWork.com allow individuals to connect with sex workers, including those catering to tourists.

Public health concerns associated with sex tourism in the UK include the transmission of sexually transmitted infections (STIs) like HIV, chlamydia, and gonorrhea. The UK's large and diverse sex work industry, especially with international sex workers, presents a risk of STI spread, compounded by a lack of consistent safety practices. There are also concerns about the exploitation of sex workers, especially those trafficked or coerced into sex work, and the associated physical and mental health issues they face. Efforts to address these concerns include regular health checks for sex workers, safer sex campaigns, and legal protections for workers, though the issue of exploitation remains prevalent.

 ## Tips to Avoid Being Solicited

To avoid being propositioned by a sex worker in the UK, it's important to **stay aware of your surroundings**, especially in areas known for sex work. Project confidence by walking purposefully and maintaining direct eye contact, as this can discourage unwanted attention. **Avoid engaging in conversation** and keep interactions brief if approached. Dressing simply and avoiding flashy clothing can also help reduce attention. Stay in well-lit, populated areas, and **avoid secluded spots**. If approached, be assertive and politely but **firmly decline**, then walk away if necessary. Understanding the legal context is key, as soliciting is illegal, and you can report harassment to the police if needed. Prioritize your safety by traveling with others or using public transport in higher-risk areas.

Law of the Land Hypothetical

HYPOTHETICAL: *John, a 28-year-old man from the United States, is visiting London for a few days. While walking through a popular area in the West End, he is approached by a woman who offers sexual services in exchange for money. John, not interested, politely declines, but he is unsure whether he could be breaking any laws simply by being approached in this manner. He wonders whether the fact that he is a tourist makes any difference in how the law applies to him.*

ANSWER: *As a visitor to the UK, John is still subject to UK laws, including those related to prostitution. Simply being approached with an offer of sexual services does not make him liable for any offense, as long as he does not engage in or solicit paid sex. However, if he had offered money for sex (solicitation), he could face prosecution, regardless of his nationality. Since he politely declined and did not engage, he hasn't broken the law. If approached again, he should refuse firmly and report any harassment to the police.*

Takeaways

- **Prostitution itself is legal** in the UK, but related activities such as brothel-keeping, soliciting in public, and pimping are illegal. The law focuses on reducing exploitation and human trafficking.

- **Prostitution Practices:** While street prostitution is in decline, indoor prostitution (brothels and escort services) and online platforms have become more common. Many sex workers now operate through escort agencies or websites, though they still face risks of exploitation and violence.

- **Sex Trafficking and Exploitation:** The UK is a destination for sex trafficking, where vulnerable individuals, often through coercion or force, are exploited for sex work. The government has laws, such as the Modern Slavery Act 2015, to combat trafficking.

- **Public Health and Sex Tourism:** The UK sees some sex tourism, especially in major cities. Public health risks include STIs like HIV and chlamydia, with concerns over the exploitation of both domestic and international sex workers.

- **Safety Tips:** To avoid being solicited, stay aware of your surroundings, project confidence, and dress simply. If approached, firmly decline and walk away. Understanding the legal context is important, as soliciting is illegal, and harassment can be reported to the police.

LGBTQ

LGBTQ

Homophobia in the UK

Historically, the UK government criminalized homosexuality, with laws such as the **Buggery Act of 1533** making same-sex acts punishable by death. Homosexuality remained illegal until the **Sexual Offences Act 1967**, which decriminalized it for consenting adults over 21 in England and Wales. Over the following decades, significant legal and social changes began, such as the repeal of **Section 28** in 2000, the equalization of the age of consent in 2001, and the introduction of **same-sex civil partnerships** in 2004, culminating in the legalization of **same-sex marriage** in 2013. These shifts marked the UK's gradual movement toward acceptance of LGBTQ+ rights.

Today, the UK is considered **one of the most LGBTQ+-friendly countries**, with widespread cultural acceptance, particularly in urban areas. Legal protections for LGBTQ+ individuals are strong, including anti-discrimination laws and marriage equality. However, attitudes can vary by region and generation, with younger people generally more accepting than older. While LGBTQ+ individuals face less legal and societal hostility, challenges such as discrimination, violence, and transphobia still persist, especially in rural areas and conservative communities.

Cultural, social, and religious factors play a significant role in shaping attitudes toward LGBTQ+ people in the UK. **Religious influences**, particularly from conservative Christian communities, often contribute to negative views, as some denominations still consider homosexuality and same-sex relationships sinful. **Cultural norms** in more traditional or rural areas can also perpetuate resistance to LGBTQ+ rights, favoring conventional family structures. Additionally, **social factors** like generational differences and education impact attitudes, with younger, more educated populations generally showing greater acceptance. Despite these challenges, broader societal trends toward secularism and increased visibility of LGBTQ+ issues have led to more progressive views overall.

Homophobic attitudes in the UK can manifest in various settings, such as the workplace, schools, and family environments. In the workplace, LGBTQ+ individuals may experience **microaggressions, unwanted comments,** or **exclusion** from team activities, sometimes leading to discrimination in promotions or leadership roles. In schools, **bullying** and **harassment** of LGBTQ+ students remain significant concerns, with reports indicating that many young people still face verbal abuse or physical attacks. In family settings, some LGBTQ+ individuals may experience rejection or estrangement, particularly in more conservative or religious households.

Reports on LGBTQ+-related violence in the UK highlight ongoing issues of discrimination and abuse. The **Stonewall Hate Crime Report** (2017) revealed that nearly one in five LGBTQ+ people had experienced a hate crime, with many reporting inadequate responses from the police. The **2018 National LGBT Survey** found that 21 percent of LGBTQ+ individuals had faced a hate crime or incident, with transgender people particularly vulnerable. The **Crime Survey for England and Wales** (2019) recorded 9,200 hate crimes based on sexual orientation and 1,900 based on gender identity, with many crimes going unreported. Transgender people face high rates of violence, including physical assaults and online abuse, with a significant rise in **transphobic hate crimes** in recent years. Despite legal protections, violence and discrimination against the LGBTQ+ community remain pressing issues in the UK.

Nevertheless, advocacy by public figures has played a crucial role in advancing LGBTQ+ rights in the UK by raising awareness, challenging prejudices, and pushing for legal and social change. Public figures like **Stephen Fry, Olly Alexander,** and **Lily Allen** have used their platforms to openly discuss LGBTQ+ issues, bringing them into the mainstream and encouraging public dialogue. Their visibility has helped normalize LGBTQ+ identities and experiences, counteracting stigma and fostering greater acceptance.

LGBTQ Legislation

The UK has a range of laws that are generally supportive of LGBTQ+ rights, reflecting significant progress over the past few decades. These laws provide **legal protections against discrimination** and **ensure equal treatment** for LGBTQ+ individuals in several areas, including employment, marriage, and public services.

Key supportive laws include the **Equality Act 2010**, which prohibits discrimination based on sexual orientation and gender identity in the workplace, education, and public services. The **Marriage (Same-Sex Couples) Act 2013** legalized same-sex marriage in England and Wales, allowing same-sex couples to marry and access the same legal rights as heterosexual couples. Additionally, the **Gender Recognition Act 2004** allows transgender individuals to change their gender on official documents, though there have been calls for reform to make this process more accessible and less bureaucratic. In recent years, the UK government has also taken steps to introduce a ban on **conversion therapy**, reflecting growing support for LGBTQ+ rights.

However, while the law offers strong protections, there are still **areas where LGBTQ+ individuals face challenges. Transgender people**, in particular, continue to face barriers, with delays in the gender recognition process and ongoing debates about **transgender rights** in society. Discrimination and hate crimes against LGBTQ+ people, especially transgender and non-binary individuals, remain persistent issues, despite legal protections.

LGBTQ Tourism and Safety Concerns

LGBTQ+ tourism is well-developed in the UK, with the country being a prominent destination for LGBTQ+ travelers. Cities like **London, Brighton**, and **Manchester** are known for their **thriving LGBTQ+ communities**, hosting popular Pride events, LGBTQ+-friendly accommodations, and vibrant nightlife. **Brighton Pride** is one of the largest and most well-known Pride festivals in the country, attracting thousands of international visitors each year. Additionally, many of the UK's historic and cultural sites are also marketed as LGBTQ+ friendly, and the UK offers a range of events, festivals, and tours catering to LGBTQ+ interests.

Public displays of affection (PDA) between LGBTQ+ visitors are generally accepted in most areas of the UK, especially in cities like **London** and **Brighton**, where LGBTQ+ rights are well-established, and attitudes are progressive. In these cities, it's common to see same-sex couples holding hands or showing affection without fear of harassment. However, in more conservative or rural areas, LGBTQ+ individuals, including visitors, might encounter less acceptance or subtle forms of discrimination. Public displays of affection are less common or more reserved in these areas, although overt hostility is relatively rare compared to some other countries.

As for **safety concerns**, the UK is predominantly considered a safe destination for LGBTQ+ visitors. However, incidents of **homophobic** or **transphobic harassment** can still occur, particularly in more rural or less progressive regions. LGBTQ+ travelers should remain vigilant in areas where cultural attitudes may be less tolerant. It's also advisable for visitors to be aware of local customs, such as respecting personal space and considering the socio-political climate in certain regions. **LGBTQ+ hate crimes** are reported, but the UK has strong legal protections, and incidents of discrimination can be reported to authorities. That said, London, Brighton, and other urban centers tend to have strong support networks, resources, and community organizations to ensure the safety and well-being of LGBTQ+ individuals.

General Questions

1. *Are there any punishments for homosexual expressions and conduct?* **No**. There are no punishments for homosexual expressions or conduct in the UK. Homosexuality was decriminalized in 1967, and since then, laws like the **Equality Act 2010** protect LGBTQ+ individuals from discrimination. The UK has legal protections for homosexual conduct, including the legalization of **same-sex marriage** in 2013, and there are no penalties for being openly homosexual.

2. *Are LGBTQ+ individuals allowed to adopt children in the UK?* **Yes**. LGBTQ+ individuals and same-sex couples are legally allowed to adopt children in the UK. The **Adoption and Children Act 2002** and subsequent legal reforms ensure that adoption decisions are made based on the best interests of the child, rather than the sexual orientation or gender identity of the adoptive parents. Same-sex couples have the same adoption rights as heterosexual couples, and LGBTQ+ individuals can adopt either as individuals or as part of a couple. This reflects the UK's commitment to equality in family law.

Law of the Land True Story[16]

As of the writing of this book, the UK Supreme Court is considering a landmark case that could significantly impact the **definition of "woman" in law**, with potential effects on gender-based rights across Scotland, England, and Wales. The case arises from a dispute between the Scottish government and the women's rights group For Women

---

16 https://apnews.com/article/
uk-supreme-court-trans-gender-case-cf2bbc911c59b147a5261f431ee93eb7

Scotland (FWS), who are challenging whether transgender women with a gender recognition certificate can be legally regarded as women under the Equality Act of 2010. FWS argues that this could affect the functioning of single-sex spaces like hospitals and sports clubs, while the Scottish government defends the inclusion of trans women, asserting that the Gender Recognition Act of 2004 entitles those with a gender recognition certificate to the same protections as those born biologically female.

The case stems from a 2018 Scottish bill mandating gender balance on public sector boards, which initially included trans women in its definition of "woman." After a court ruling in favor of the Scottish government, FWS brought the case to the Supreme Court, seeking clarity on the legal meaning of "sex" under the Equality Act. Both sides presented compelling arguments: FWS emphasized the importance of protecting biological sex rights, while the Scottish government stressed that a gender recognition certificate was a fundamental legal status change. The court's final ruling, expected soon, could have far-reaching implications for the rights of trans individuals and the operation of gender-specific services.

 ## Law of the Land Hypothetical

HYPOTHETICAL: *Sophie, a transgender woman, recently transitioned and now works as a software developer for a large tech company in London. She has updated her gender on all official documents, including her passport, driver's license, and medical records. Sophie applies for a promotion to a senior role in her company, but her application is rejected. She suspects that her gender identity was a factor in the decision, although the company claims the decision was based on qualifications and performance. Does Sophie have legal grounds to claim discrimination under UK law, and if so, what legal protections exist for transgender individuals in the workplace?*

ANSWER: **Yes.** *Sophie may have legal grounds to claim discrimination under UK law. The **Equality Act 2010** protects transgender* *individuals from discrimination in the workplace, including on the grounds of gender reassignment. This protection applies regardless of whether Sophie has undergone medical transition. If Sophie believes her promotion was denied due to her transgender status, she can pursue a claim for* **discrimination.**

Employers are required to ensure a workplace free from discrimination based on sex or gender reassignment. Sophie can file a grievance with her employer, and if unresolved, bring a case before an employment tribunal. If she can show that her qualifications were comparable to other candidates and that her gender identity influenced the decision, she may be entitled to compensation or even a promotion.

CHAPTER 9

SEXUALLY MOTIVATED/ VIOLENT CRIMES

SEXUALLY MOTIVATED/ VIOLENT CRIMES

Overview

Sexually motivated crimes, including sexual assault, harassment, and rape, continue to be a **significant issue** in the UK, with reports indicating an increase in such offenses. According to the Office for National Statistics (ONS), more than 160,000 sexual offenses were recorded by the police in 2023, a figure that has been rising over the years. However, it's widely believed that the actual number of incidents is likely much higher, as many cases go unreported due to fear of stigma, lack of trust in the justice system, or victims' personal circumstances.

Several social, cultural, and economic factors contribute to the prevalence of sexually motivated crimes. **Societal attitudes** toward gender and power dynamics can perpetuate harmful norms that lead to victim-blaming and a culture of silence around sexual violence. Traditional views on gender roles, particularly in more conservative regions, can also hinder efforts to combat these crimes. **Economic factors**, such as poverty, homelessness, and social inequality, play a significant role in making certain groups, particularly women and marginalized individuals, more vulnerable to sexual violence. The growing use of **technology** has introduced new challenges, with crimes like revenge porn, online harassment, and sexual exploitation becoming more prevalent on digital platforms.

Women are the most affected by sexually motivated crimes in the UK, with studies revealing that about one in five women have experienced some form of sexual assault since the age of 16. **Transgender and gender-nonconforming individuals** also face disproportionately high rates of sexual violence, often due to their marginalized status and the heightened discrimination they face. **Young people**, particularly those aged 16 to 24, are also at higher risk of experiencing sexual violence, with incidents of date rape and sexual harassment being more common in this age group.

There are **regional differences** in the prevalence of sexual crimes. Larger urban centers, such as London, Manchester, and Birmingham, report higher rates of sexual offenses, likely due to their larger populations and greater access to reporting mechanisms. However, rural areas, despite having less reported cases, may have a different problem: underreporting. The stigma and isolation often found in smaller communities can prevent victims from coming forward, leaving many cases unaddressed.

Despite the increasing awareness and legal protections for victims, sexual crimes remain a complex and pervasive issue in the UK, shaped by a variety of cultural, social, and economic factors. Although progress has been made, much work remains to ensure that those affected by such crimes receive the support and justice they deserve.

Related Legislation

In the UK, legislative protection against sexually motivated crimes is robust, with various laws designed to safeguard victims and punish perpetrators. The **Sexual Offences Act 2003** is the cornerstone of the UK's legal framework for addressing sexual violence. This Act criminalizes a wide range of offenses, including rape, sexual assault, and harassment, and sets out the legal definition of consent, making it clear that individuals must provide voluntary and informed consent for sexual activity. It also expanded the definition of rape to include penetration with an object, ensuring that the law encompasses a wider range of sexual crimes.

Additionally, the **Domestic Abuse Act 2021** includes provisions that protect victims from sexual violence in the context of intimate partner relationships, making it illegal to engage in sexual activity without consent, even within marriage or cohabiting relationships. This Act further strengthened the legal tools available to address sexual violence, making provisions for the use of "Revenge Porn" laws and expanding the scope of behavior considered abusive under the law.

There are also legal measures to protect vulnerable individuals, such as those who are intoxicated or under the age of consent. **The age of consent in the UK is 16**, and any sexual activity with someone below that age is considered statutory rape. The law also provides specific protections for people with mental disabilities or cognitive impairments, ensuring that they cannot be coerced into sexual activity.

Penalties for those convicted of sexually motivated crimes are **severe**. **Rape**, for example, carries a **maximum sentence of life imprisonment**, while **sexual assault** can result in sentences of **up to ten years**, depending on the severity of the offense. Offenders may also face **mandatory registration as sex offenders**, which carries a range of restrictions, including being prohibited from working with children or vulnerable adults. Repeat offenders and those convicted of particularly heinous crimes, such as multiple assaults, can face even harsher sentences.

Enforcement, however, remains an area of concern. While there are strict laws in place, the **conviction rate** for sexual offenses in the UK is **relatively low**. According to the Crown Prosecution Service (CPS), fewer than 2 percent of reported rapes result in a conviction. This is partly due to challenges in gathering sufficient evidence, as sexual offenses often lack witnesses and forensic evidence, as well as a reluctance from victims to come forward due to the trauma involved in reporting such crimes. The "Victims' Code," which ensures that victims of sexual offenses receive support throughout the legal process, aims to address these gaps, but it remains a challenge to ensure that all victims have equal access to justice.

In recent years, there have been efforts to improve enforcement through the creation of specialized police units and training programs aimed at investigating sexual offenses more effectively. However, significant improvements are still needed, particularly in addressing the widespread issue of underreporting and ensuring that perpetrators face justice more consistently.

General Questions

1. *Do laws in the UK related to sex crimes protect the victims equally?* **Yes.** UK laws related to sex crimes are designed to protect all victims equally, regardless of gender, sexual orientation, or identity. The law focuses on the consent of the victim and criminalizes acts of sexual assault, harassment, and exploitation. For example, both men and women can be victims of rape or sexual assault under the Sexual Offences Act 2003. The law also acknowledges that victims may experience different forms of trauma based on their background, and it provides measures to support vulnerable individuals. However, some advocacy groups argue that there are disparities in how victims are treated, particularly in cases involving LGBTQ+ individuals or people from marginalized communities

2. *Pursuant to law, what is the age of consent for sex in UK?* In the UK, the **legal age of consent** for sexual activity is **16 years old**. This applies regardless of gender or sexual orientation. However, there are specific laws that protect young people, such as restrictions on adults in positions of trust (teachers, care workers, etc.), who may not legally engage in sexual activity with individuals under 18. Additionally, the law also protects against exploitation, with specific regulations for those under the age of 16, as sexual activity with someone below this age is automatically deemed illegal.

Law of the Land Hypothetical

HYPOTHETICAL: *Sophie works in an office environment with her colleague, Tom. Over the past few months, Tom has repeatedly sent Sophie personal messages on social media, commenting on her appearance and making jokes about her private life. Sophie has asked Tom to stop multiple times, but he continues to make these comments both in person and online. Sophie feels increasingly uncomfortable and intimidated by Tom's behavior. Can Tom be legally charged with harassment, and what steps can Sophie take to address this behavior under UK law?*

ANSWER: *Yes. Tom's behavior may qualify as harassment under UK law. The **Protection from Harassment Act 1997** makes it an offense to engage in a course of conduct that causes distress or alarm. Tom's repeated unwanted messages and comments, despite Sophie's objections, could be considered harassment. Sophie can report the issue to HR, as the company is obligated to address harassment in the workplace. She should also keep evidence of all messages and interactions. If HR doesn't take appropriate action, Sophie could pursue legal recourse under the Protection from Harassment Act 1997, which could include seeking a civil injunction or criminal charges. In severe cases, she may be entitled to compensation for emotional distress.*

 **Takeaways**

- Sexually motivated crimes are a growing concern in the UK, with many incidents going unreported due to stigma or lack of trust in the justice system.

- Legislation offers robust protections for victims of sexual violence, with key laws like the Sexual Offences Act 2003 and the Domestic Abuse Act 2021 ensuring that sexual assault, harassment, and rape are criminalized, and consent is clearly defined.

- Vulnerable groups, including women, transgender individuals, and young people, are disproportionately affected by sexually motivated crimes, with societal, economic, and cultural factors contributing to their vulnerability.

- The age of consent in the UK is 16, with special legal protections for those in positions of trust and for young people, as any sexual activity with someone under this age is considered statutory rape.

- Underreporting and low conviction rates remain significant challenges, with fewer than 2 percent of reported rapes resulting in convictions, despite legal safeguards and growing awareness.

ARRESTED IN THE UK

CHAPTER 10

ARRESTED IN THE UK

Overview

When traveling in a foreign country, it's imperative to recognize that you are subject to the legal jurisdiction and regulations of that nation. These laws may significantly differ from those in your home country and might not offer the same legal protections you are accustomed to. It's crucial to bear in mind that penalties for violating foreign laws can be more severe than those for similar offenses in your home country, and ignorance of these laws is not typically accepted as a defense.

The consequences for breaking the law while abroad can be severe and may include expulsion, fines, arrest, or imprisonment. Even unintentional violations can lead to serious legal repercussions. It is essential for travelers to be aware of and adhere to the laws of the host country to avoid legal entanglements and ensure a safe and enjoyable experience.

Specifically, stringent penalties are often enforced for possession, use, or trafficking of illegal drugs in many countries. Convicted offenders can expect severe consequences, including lengthy jail sentences and hefty fines. The legal processes for foreigners in the event of an arrest abroad involve being charged or indicted, prosecuted, potentially convicted and sentenced, and, if applicable, going through an appeals process.

Navigating a foreign legal system can be complex, and individuals arrested abroad must be prepared to comply with the legal procedures of the host country. Seeking legal representation and understanding the local legal nuances are crucial steps for those facing legal issues in a foreign jurisdiction.

Awareness of and adherence to the laws of a foreign country are paramount when traveling. Understanding the potential consequences for legal violations and being prepared to navigate the legal system of the host country are essential aspects of responsible international travel.

Arrest Process[17]

In the UK, the arrest process is governed by specific laws and procedures aimed at ensuring that the rights of the arrested person are respected while also maintaining public safety. When a police officer arrests an individual in the UK, they must inform the person of the **reason for the arrest** and the charges, unless informing them would hinder the investigation or cause harm to the public. In general, the following steps occur:

1. Police officers have the authority to arrest someone if they have **"reasonable grounds"** to believe that the person has committed a crime or is about to commit one. Arrests can also occur if the individual is suspected of breaching bail conditions.

2. Once arrested, the individual must be informed of their rights. The police will issue a **"caution,"** which is a statement informing the individual of their right to remain silent and their right to have legal representation (this is often referred to as the **"right to silence"** caution). The caution usually goes "You do not have to say anything, but it may harm your defense if you do not mention when questioned something which you later rely on in court. Anything you do say may be used in evidence."

3. Police are allowed to use reasonable force if the person resists arrest or tries to flee. Excessive force is not permitted.

---

17 https://www.noblesolicitors.co.uk/about/a-guide-to-police-station-procedures.html

After the arrest, the individual will be taken to a police station where they will be **booked into custody**. They will be searched, their personal details recorded, and they may be fingerprinted and photographed. The arrested individual will be **interviewed** by the police. The interviews are typically recorded. During questioning, the suspect has the right to remain silent and should have access to a solicitor. If they waive the right to remain silent, anything they say can be used as evidence. Following the interview, the individual may be released **with conditions** (e.g., to return to court on a specific date) or **without bail**, depending on the severity of the crime.

If sufficient evidence is gathered, the individual may be formally charged and brought before a court. If the crime is serious and there are concerns that the person might flee or commit further crimes, they can be kept in **detention** while investigations continue. However, after **24 hours** of detention, a person must either be charged or released unless a magistrate grants an extension for a longer detention. If charged, the person must appear before a **magistrate's court**. For more serious offenses, the case may be transferred to the Crown Court. During the hearing, the defendant will **enter a plea**, and the court will decide on bail conditions and trial procedures.

Rights of the Arrested Person[18]

In the UK, individuals who are arrested are entitled to a range of **legal protections** designed to ensure their rights are respected during the arrest and subsequent legal proceedings. These protections are enshrined in various laws, primarily the **Police and Criminal Evidence Act 1984 (PACE)**, the **Human Rights Act 1998**, and other related legislation. They include:

Right to be Informed of the Reason for Arrest:

Upon arrest, an individual must be informed of the reason for their arrest **as soon as possible**. This is a basic right to ensure the person

---

18   https://www.gov.uk/arrested-your-rights

understands the charges or suspicions against them. If this isn't done immediately, the arrest may be deemed unlawful.

Right to Legal Representation (Access to a Solicitor):

An arrested person has the right to legal representation. They can choose a solicitor to help with their case. If the individual cannot afford a solicitor, they are entitled to free legal advice through the Legal Aid system. Police must inform the individual of their right to speak to a solicitor in private, and they are usually given the opportunity to consult with a lawyer before the interview process begins.

Right to Remain Silent:

The person being arrested has the right to remain silent. Anything they say during the interview may be used as evidence, so they are entitled to not answer questions without legal representation. However, a refusal to answer questions may negatively impact the person's defense later in court, but they cannot be forced to speak.

Right to be Informed of the Right to Silence:

The arrested person must be told of their right to remain silent and their right to consult a solicitor. This caution is provided to ensure that the individual understands their rights at the point of arrest.

Right to be Brought Before a Court:

After arrest, an individual has the right to be brought before a court **within 24 hours** (unless it is a serious crime, and a magistrate permits longer detention). If charges are not brought or if the individual is not presented in court within this time frame, they must be released.

Right to an Interpreter:

If the arrested person does not speak or understand English, they have the right to an interpreter during questioning and legal proceedings. The police are required to arrange for an interpreter, ensuring that the person understands the charges and their rights during the investigation.

Right to be Treated Fairly and Humanely:

Under the **Human Rights Act 1998**, everyone, including those arrested, is entitled to be treated with dignity and respect. Police must ensure that the arrested person is not subjected to inhumane treatment or abuse. Arrested individuals should not be subject to unnecessary detention or excessive force. They should be provided with adequate food, water, and access to basic hygiene facilities, and their health should be monitored.

Protection Against Unlawful Detention:

A person can only be detained for a limited period without being charged. If they are not charged within a reasonable time (usually 24 hours for most offenses, or up to 96 hours for serious crimes like terrorism), they must be released. Detention beyond this period requires judicial oversight. A magistrate or court can grant an extension for detention.

Right to Access to Family or Friends:

An arrested individual is generally allowed to inform someone (usually a family member or friend) of their arrest. This right can be delayed in exceptional circumstances, but police must record the reasons for any delay.

Foreign nationals who are arrested in the UK are entitled to the same fundamental rights and protections as UK citizens. However, there are some **special considerations** that apply specifically to foreign nationals:[19]

Right to Contact a Consular Official:

Foreign nationals arrested in the UK have the right to contact their embassy or consulate. If they request, the police must notify the relevant consular authorities, who may assist the individual in obtaining legal advice or support. This is a protection under **international law**, ensuring that the foreign national is not deprived of consular assistance.

Interpreter Services:

If the foreign national does not understand or speak English, they have the right to an interpreter. The police are required to provide an interpreter to ensure the individual understands their rights, the charges against them, and the legal process.

Access to Legal Representation:

Foreign nationals are entitled to the same access to legal representation as UK citizens. They may also have the right to legal assistance in their own language. If the foreign national cannot afford legal representation, they may qualify for **Legal Aid** in the UK, depending on the circumstances.

Right to Remain Silent and Fair Trial:

Foreign nationals are afforded the same legal rights, including the right to remain silent and the right to a fair trial. However, in some cases, depending on the individual's country of origin, diplomatic negotiations

---

19   https://www.makwanas.co.uk/
     my-rights-if-im-a-foreign-national-arrested-in-the-uk/

or concerns about their treatment in their home country could influence their case.

Deportation:

If a foreign national is convicted of a serious crime in the UK, they could face deportation after serving their sentence. Deportation laws can be applied based on the severity of the crime and whether the individual is a risk to public safety. For example, foreign nationals involved in drug trafficking, serious assault, or terrorism-related offenses may be deported upon completion of their prison sentence.

International Warrants:

Foreign nationals in the UK who are subject to arrest under an international warrant (such as an arrest warrant issued by another country) may be extradited to their home country. This process is governed by treaties and international law, and extradition requests are typically handled by the **Home Office** or through a magistrate's court.

If you are a foreign national and get arrested while in the UK, you should notify your embassy or consulate immediately. They can help contact family, friends, or employers of the detained U.S. citizen with their written consent, visit the detained U.S. citizen in jail, help ensure that prison officials provide appropriate medical care, explain the local criminal justice and legal processes, and most importantly, connect you to local attorneys. Bear in mind, however, that their powers are limited and they cannot get U.S. citizens out of jail, provide legal advice or represent U.S. citizens in court, serve as official interpreters or translators, nor can they pay your legal, medical, or other fees.

Getting Legal Assistance

If you find yourself arrested while in the United Kingdom, the first step is to **remain calm** and **cooperative**. Your behavior during the arrest can significantly influence the situation and potential outcomes. Inform the arresting officers that you are a foreign national and request to contact your country's embassy or consulate. Under international law, you are entitled to have your **consulate** notified of your arrest. This notification is vital, as it helps ensure you receive the necessary support, including assistance in securing legal representation and understanding the UK's legal processes.

For British citizens or foreign nationals requiring assistance, you can contact the consular services at your embassy. The UK embassy or consulate can assist in several ways, including contacting family, friends, or employers (with your consent), providing guidance on your legal rights, ensuring that you have access to proper healthcare in detention, and connecting you with local English-speaking lawyers.

However, it's important to note that **consular assistance is limited**. While the embassy can provide support, they cannot intervene directly in legal matters, offer legal advice or representation in court, act as interpreters, or cover your legal, medical, or other expenses.

For more information or to get in touch with local resources, visit the website of the nearest embassy or consulate in the UK.

Bail[20]

The UK has a bail system, but it works differently than in some other countries, particularly the United States. The bail system in the UK is governed by several key pieces of legislation, including the **Police and Criminal Evidence Act 1984** (**PACE**) and **The Bail Act 1976**. The main purpose of the system is to allow individuals arrested for an offense to be released while awaiting trial, but with conditions that ensure their attendance in court and reduce the risk of further crimes.

After an individual is arrested, they can be taken into police custody. The police have the discretion to release the individual on bail or keep them in custody while they conduct further investigations or gather evidence.

---

20 https://www.cps.gov.uk/legal-guidance/bail

In cases where **bail** is **granted**, it can either be **unconditional**, meaning the person is released without further restrictions, or **conditional**, where specific terms must be followed such as requiring the person to report to the police at a specific time, restrict their travel, or have them stay at a particular address. If bail conditions are violated, the accused could face additional charges or be detained. If bail is **refused**, the accused will be remanded in custody until their trial.

Bail can be **reviewed** in certain situations. If it is initially denied, the person may apply for a bail review, typically through a higher court, which will re-examine the decision. If the judge feels it is appropriate, they may grant bail or alter the conditions.

Tourists and foreign nationals have similar rights to UK citizens when it comes to bail. However, there are **additional considerations for visitors**. Foreign nationals are often seen as higher flight risks because they may not have strong ties to the UK. This can result in **stricter conditions**, such as the surrender of passports or restrictions on travel. Visitors may also be asked to stay at a specific address or report to the police more frequently. In some cases, bail may be denied entirely if the court believes the individual could leave the country before trial or if the offense is particularly serious.

Complaints Against Police

The general reputation of the UK police force is **mixed**, with **significant public trust** but **also notable criticisms**. In general, the police in the UK are seen as professional, approachable, and well-trained. However, there have been a number of high-profile cases of misconduct, controversial policing practices, and issues with accountability that have tarnished their reputation in some areas.

The UK police are often praised for their ability to deal with a wide range of public safety issues, their responsiveness to emergency situations, and their commitment to preventing crime. Many people have positive experiences with the police, particularly in relation to the support offered during emergencies or in dealing with incidents of violence, theft, or public disorder.

However, the UK police force is not without criticism, and the most common complaints tend to revolve around issues of police misconduct, discrimination, and poor handling of certain situations.

One of the most significant complaints relates to **racial profiling and discrimination.** Several ethnic minority groups, especially Black, Asian, and other non-white communities, report feeling disproportionately targeted by police. This includes higher rates of stop and search, perceived biased treatment, and higher levels of scrutiny. Despite efforts to tackle racism within the force, reports from organizations like the Independent Office for Police Conduct (IOPC) and community groups indicate that racial disparities persist, which contributes to distrust in the police from some communities.

Use of force is another major area of concern. There have been numerous complaints about the excessive use of force by the police, particularly in **public demonstrations** or encounters with **people from marginalized communities.** Instances of police officers using force disproportionately in situations involving unarmed individuals, particularly young people and people of color, have led to criticisms of a lack of appropriate de-escalation techniques and training.

Another common area of criticism is the **handling of domestic violence and sexual assault cases.** The police have been accused of mishandling cases, failing to adequately investigate or provide proper support to victims. In some cases, reports of domestic violence have been dismissed, not taken seriously, or inadequately handled. There have been concerns about police not doing enough to prevent **violence against women** or holding perpetrators accountable, with some victims feeling that their complaints are minimized. Additionally, **corruption and misconduct within the force** have also been notable sources of public discontent. While not widespread, there have been instances of police officers engaging in unethical behavior, including **bribery, misuse of power,** and **cover-ups.** The **Daniel Morgan case** (see Law of the Land True Story below) and other examples of police corruption have fueled public concern about accountability and oversight.

A longstanding issue in the British police force is **failure to address complaints effectively**. Some members of the public believe that when complaints are made against officers, there is often a lack of transparency and accountability. There have been reports of internal investigations being insufficient or biased, and this has eroded public confidence in how seriously complaints are taken.

How to File a Complaint Against the Police

Filing a complaint against the police in the UK involves a clear, structured process aimed at holding officers accountable for any misconduct or negligence. The first step is to identify the nature of your complaint, whether it's related to unprofessional behavior, excessive force, failure to investigate a crime, or any other form of misconduct.

Once you've determined the issue, the next step is to contact the police force involved. Most police forces have a **formal process for complaints**, which usually includes a dedicated complaints unit. You can file a complaint **directly with the police force** in person, by phone, or online. Many police forces have complaint forms on their websites, which allow you to submit your complaint digitally. If you prefer, you can also send a written complaint by post or call the complaints department to report your issue.

If you are dissatisfied with how the police force handles your complaint or if the issue is particularly serious, you can escalate the matter to the **Independent Office for Police Conduct (IOPC)**. The IOPC is an independent body that investigates serious complaints, such as police brutality, death in custody, or other severe incidents of misconduct. You can submit a complaint directly to the IOPC via their website or by phone. They will assess your case and determine if further investigation is necessary.

When submitting a complaint, it's important to provide as much detail as possible. Include the date, time, and location of the incident, along with the names or badge numbers of any officers involved, if known. A detailed account of the events leading to your complaint is essential, and you should also include any supporting evidence such as photos, videos, or witness statements. Complaints must typically be made **within 12 months** of the incident. If the complaint is filed after this time, the police may still consider it, but they may decide not to investigate if they believe it's too late. After the complaint is filed, the police or the IOPC will review it. If the issue is minor, the police may offer an apology or resolve the matter informally. However, if the complaint is serious, it will be investigated, and you will be informed of the outcome. If you're unhappy with the decision, you can appeal either to the IOPC or, in some cases, the **Police Appeals Tribunal**.

Throughout this process, various organizations, such as **Liberty**, **Inquest**, and the **Police Federation**, offer support and advice. These organizations can guide you through the complaint process, help you understand your rights, and ensure that your complaint is handled properly. Making a complaint against the police is your right, and if you feel the police aren't responding appropriately, you can escalate the matter for further review and potential investigation.

 ## Law of the Land True Story[21]

The Daniel Morgan murder case has been a prolonged battle for justice that lasted over 30 years. In March 1987, Daniel Morgan, a private detective, was found murdered with an axe in a south London pub car park. The investigation was plagued by police corruption and incompetence, and no one was ever convicted. The Morgan family believed Daniel was for his intent to expose a corrupt police network.

In July 2023, the Metropolitan Police and the Morgan family reached a settlement, with the police admitting responsibility for the failures in the case. Met Commissioner Sir Mark Rowley acknowledged the corruption and systemic issues within the force that hindered the investigation. He publicly apologized to the Morgan family for their prolonged suffering.

---

21 https://www.theguardian.com/uk-news/2023/jul/19/daniel-morgan-met-admits-failings-and-pays-damages-in-settlement-with-family

An official inquiry in 2021 found the Met Police was institutionally corrupt, prioritizing its reputation over seeking justice. Despite the settlement, which included a £2.25m payout and an apology, no officers faced formal consequences. The family continues to fight for justice, and the Metropolitan Police has vowed to keep investigating, offering a reward for information.

General Questions

1. *If I am convicted in the UK, am I likely to be released on bail pending the outcome of my appeal?* In the UK, being granted bail pending an appeal depends on several factors. The court will consider whether the appeal has a realistic chance of success, the seriousness of the offense, and the risk of reoffending or fleeing. If the conviction involves a serious crime, bail is less likely to be granted. If bail is granted, conditions such as reporting to the police or wearing an electronic tag may be imposed. Ultimately, the court weighs the likelihood of the appeal's success and any potential risks to public safety.

2. *What influences a bail determination?* In the UK, several factors influence a bail determination. The court will consider whether there is a significant risk that the defendant may abscond, commit further offenses, or interfere with witnesses. The seriousness of the offense, the likelihood of a conviction, and the defendant's previous criminal record are also taken into account. Additionally, if the defendant has strong community ties, employment, or family connections, this may work in their favor.

3. *If I am arrested, how soon will I see a judge or magistrate?*
When arrested, you are entitled to be brought before a judge or
magistrate as soon as reasonably possible. If you are arrested
and held in custody, the law stipulates that you must be brought
before a magistrates' court **within 24 hours,** excluding weekends and bank holidays. In certain cases, a judge may extend the
detention period for more serious offenses, but they must review
the decision regularly.

4. *Will I be able to contact my country's embassy in the UK?*
Yes. If you are arrested in the UK, you have the right to contact
your country's embassy or consulate. This right is protected under international agreements and is generally upheld by UK authorities. The police are required to inform you of this right, and
they must allow you to make reasonable arrangements to contact
your embassy, especially if you're a foreign national. However,
this contact may be subject to certain practical limitations, such
as ensuring that the contact doesn't interfere with police procedures or investigations.

JAILS VS. PRISONS: CONDITIONS & CULTURE

JAILS VS. PRISONS: CONDITIONS & CULTURE

Overview

In the UK, the terms *jail* and *prison* are often used interchangeably, but they refer to different types of facilities within the criminal justice system. **Jails**, also known **as remand centers** or **custody suites**, are **temporary detention facilities**. They are used primarily for individuals who have been arrested and are awaiting trial or sentencing, or those serving short sentences, typically less than 12 months. **Prisons**, on the other hand, are **long-term facilities** for individuals who have been convicted and sentenced to imprisonment. They house inmates serving sentences **longer than 12 months**.

Prisons in the UK are operated by the government under the **Ministry of Justice**, while jails are typically managed by local police authorities or private companies contracted to run remand centers. Prisons are categorized by their **level of security**, such as Category A (high security), Category B (medium security), Category C (low security), and Category D (open prisons). In contrast, jails generally do not have the same levels of categorization but may be equipped to handle different levels of risk based on the detainee's status (e.g., remand prisoners or those awaiting trial).

One of the biggest challenges facing the UK's jail and prison system is **overcrowding**. Overcrowding leads to poor living conditions, strained resources, and heightened tensions among inmates and staff. **Budget cuts** have further exacerbated these issues, leading to a reduction in rehabilitation programs and staff shortages. This has created difficulties in maintaining order and providing inmates with the support they need to reintegrate into society.

The UK prison system offers a variety of initiatives aimed at reducing reoffending and promoting the rehabilitation of offenders. These programs include educational courses, vocational training, mental health services, substance abuse programs, and therapeutic interventions designed to address underlying issues like anger management or family dynamics. Some prisons also offer work programs where inmates can develop skills that might help them find employment after their release. However, the availability and effectiveness of these programs vary depending on the type of prison and available resources. In recent years, critics have highlighted that while rehabilitation is theoretically a core objective of the system, budget cuts, overcrowding, and staff shortages have hindered the ability to offer comprehensive support to inmates.

Prison Conditions and Living Environment

Living conditions in UK prisons vary depending on the type of prison (high-security, medium-security, or open prisons), as well as factors such as overcrowding, maintenance, and funding. **Overcrowding** is a persistent problem in the UK prison system, which leads to a range of negative outcomes, including reduced personal space for inmates, a lack of privacy, and increased tension within the prison population. In some prisons, multiple inmates may be forced to share small cells, often with limited space for personal belongings and privacy. These conditions can contribute to feelings of frustration, anxiety, and aggression among prisoners, making it harder to maintain order and safety within the facility.

In addition to overcrowding, the age and state of the physical **infrastructure** in some prisons also present challenges. Older prisons may suffer from poor maintenance, including issues with heating, ventilation, plumbing, and electricity, which can lead to discomfort and unsafe living conditions.

Access to healthcare in UK prisons is a right for all inmates, and healthcare services are provided through the National Health Service (NHS). The types of care available include general medical services, dental care, mental health support, and specialized treatments for chronic illnesses, substance abuse, and infectious diseases. Prisoners also have access to mental health services, which are critical given the high rates of mental health issues in the prison population, including depression, anxiety, and self-harm. However, access to healthcare in prisons faces **significant challenges**.

One of the main issues is the strain on resources. **Overcrowding** in prisons means that healthcare staff, including doctors, nurses, and mental health professionals, are often stretched thin and may struggle to meet the high demand for services. Waiting times for appointments, particularly for non-urgent care or specialist services, can be long. Additionally, there are concerns about the quality and timeliness of mental health support, with inmates sometimes waiting months to see a specialist or receive treatment for conditions such as PTSD, substance use disorders, or depression.

Prisons also face challenges in dealing with specific health needs, such as substance abuse problems, particularly drug addiction. Despite various rehabilitation programs, the high prevalence of substance use among inmates means that prisons must also address issues related to withdrawal, addiction treatment, and the prevention of drug smuggling.

Food, Sanitation, and Basic Needs

Prisons in the UK are required by law to provide inmates with food that meets basic nutritional standards, but complaints about the quality and quantity of meals are common. Some inmates report that food portions are small, poorly prepared, and lack variety. Additionally, food is sometimes seen as nutritionally inadequate, leading to health concerns over time. Overcrowding can further exacerbate issues related to food distribution, as the need to serve large numbers of prisoners at specific times can result in delays or food shortages.

Sanitation in prisons is another key concern. The UK prison system is obligated to provide inmates with access to toilets, showers, and cleaning supplies. However, overcrowding often leads to inadequate sanitation facilities, with some inmates reporting a lack of hot water, insufficient cleaning materials, or toilets that are not adequately maintained. In some cases, prisoners have complained about broken plumbing, unsanitary conditions in cells, and a general lack of hygiene standards, which can lead to the spread of diseases and infections.

Basic needs such as **clothing, bedding,** and **personal hygiene products** are also provided to inmates. While these provisions are generally met, concerns have been raised about the quality and adequacy of such items, particularly in older or underfunded institutions. For instance, inmates sometimes report receiving insufficient or poorly made clothing and bedding, which can lead to discomfort and a sense of neglect.

Inmate Rights and Legal Protections[22]

In the UK, prisoners retain certain constitutional rights, although these are significantly restricted due to their incarceration. They are entitled to basic rights such as the **right to life, freedom from torture**, and the **right to practice their religion.** Inmates also retain the **right to access legal representation, receive family visits,** and **communicate with legal advisors.** However, their rights to freedom of movement and voting are limited, and their access to the media and protests is restricted.

Access to legal resources is a key right for prisoners, including the ability to challenge their conviction, sentence, or treatment. Prisons are required to provide law libraries, legal advice, and support, although in practice, access can be limited due to overcrowding and resource constraints. Inmates can apply to the courts for various legal matters, such as appeals, judicial reviews, or complaints about their treatment. Despite these rights, legal recourse can be difficult due to barriers like limited resources and the complexity of the legal system.

---

22 https://www.gov.uk/life-in-prison/prisoner-privileges-and-rights

Abuse within the prison system is a significant concern, with prisoners sometimes facing mistreatment or violence from staff or other inmates. They have the **right to file complaints**, but these can often be met with delays, retaliation, or inadequate investigations. Legal recourse for abuse includes filing complaints with oversight bodies or suing the government for damages, but pursuing these claims can be difficult due to fear of reprisals and institutional shortcomings. Despite existing mechanisms, critics argue that abuse is often underreported and inadequately addressed, requiring continued advocacy for reform.

General Questions

1. *What is the difference between a jail and prison in the UK?* In the UK, jails (remand centers) are for individuals awaiting trial or serving short sentences (less than 12 months). Prisons are for convicted individuals serving longer sentences (over 12 months) and are categorized by security levels, from high (Category A) to open (Category D).

2. *Do jails and prisons offer religious services to inmates?* Yes. Both jails and prisons offer religious services. Chaplains provide spiritual support, organize services, and offer counseling for inmates of all faiths. Religious texts and observances of religious holidays are also provided.

3. *How do prisoners spend their time?* Prisoners spend their time engaging in work, educational programs, vocational training, physical exercise, and recreational activities. Programs may vary by facility, and access can be limited by overcrowding or security classification. Some prisons offer additional services like mental health support or addiction treatment.

4. *What type of jobs can inmates perform?* In the UK, inmates can perform various jobs aimed at providing skills for reintegration into society. These roles include maintenance tasks, such as cleaning and repairing prison facilities, working in the kitchen to prepare meals, handling laundry services, and participating in manufacturing or agricultural work, where they may produce goods or work on farms. In some prisons, inmates may also take on administrative tasks. These jobs help inmates develop vocational skills and earn small wages, which are deposited into a personal account for commissary purchases. The availability of work depends on the prison and is often combined with rehabilitative or educational programs.

5. *How does the prison commissary system work in the UK?* In the UK, the prison commissary system allows inmates to purchase additional items beyond what is provided by the prison, such as snacks, toiletries, clothing, and phone credit. These items are typically bought with money deposited into the inmate's personal account by family or friends. The commissary system helps inmates maintain some autonomy, though the prices can be higher than in the outside world. Inmates are given a weekly allowance based on their job status, and this can be used for purchasing items from the prison shop.

6. *What type of medical care do prisoners receive?* Prisoners in the UK receive medical care through the National Health Service (NHS), which operates within the prison system. Medical services include access to doctors, nurses, dentists, and mental health professionals. Inmates can request healthcare services, which are usually provided in prison clinics. For more serious health concerns, prisoners may be transferred to external hospitals. However, there have been concerns about delays in care and the quality of services due to overcrowding and budget constraints.

7. ***What is prison culture in the UK?*** Prison culture in the UK can vary between establishments, but it generally revolves around a hierarchy, with established social structures and unwritten rules. Inmates often form groups or alliances for protection or mutual support. There can be a strong sense of loyalty and trust among those within these groups. Violence, bullying, and intimidation can be prevalent, particularly in higher-security facilities. The prison staff also play a significant role in shaping the culture, with different approaches to discipline and rehabilitation impacting how inmates interact.

HELPING A FRIEND OR RELATIVE IMPRISONED IN THE UK

HELPING A FRIEND OR RELATIVE IMPRISONED IN THE UK

Overview

If a family member or friend is imprisoned while traveling in the UK, there are several important steps you should take to ensure they receive the appropriate support and assistance.

First, you should **contact the local authorities** where the person is being held. In the UK, when someone is arrested, the police must inform the detainee of their right to contact their embassy or consulate. If you're unsure where they are, you can reach out to the nearest police station to confirm the location and learn more about the charges they face. It is crucial to **get in touch with your country's embassy or consulate** in the UK. Embassies have an emergency contact service that operates 24/7, and they can help you navigate the situation. They can provide a list of local criminal lawyers, although they cannot provide legal representation or advice. The embassy can also visit your family member or friend to ensure they are treated fairly, offer interpretation services if needed, and help facilitate communication between the detained person and their family. They may also check on the conditions of detention to ensure that your loved one is not being mistreated.

The UK's legal system may differ from what you are used to, so **understanding the process is essential**. Once arrested, the detainee will be brought to a police station and informed of their rights. The person can be held for up to 24 hours (excluding weekends) before appearing in court. Depending on the severity of the charges, they may be granted bail or remain in custody until the court hearing. The embassy can assist with arranging legal counsel if needed and can offer guidance on the process.

Legal representation is key. If your family member or friend has not already **secured a lawyer**, you should help them find one. The embassy can provide a list of qualified solicitors who specialize in criminal law. If your loved one cannot afford a lawyer, the UK has a duty solicitor scheme that provides free legal representation to those who meet the eligibility criteria. This ensures that they have access to fair representation, regardless of financial means.

Staying involved and keeping in contact with the embassy and legal representatives is crucial throughout the process. They will provide updates and ensure your loved one's legal rights are upheld. If the detainee has medical or psychological needs, the embassy can help coordinate care. It's also important to keep track of the documentation and any legal proceedings as the case progresses.

In addition to legal and embassy assistance, you may need to **consider financial support**. If your loved one is required to pay bail, fines, or legal fees, the embassy can provide guidance on how to send money securely. They can also assist in transferring funds if needed. Finally, remember that the legal system in the UK, while fair, may take time. The court system is typically thorough, and delays are not uncommon. Patience and communication with the embassy, legal counsel, and local authorities will help ensure the process is as smooth as possible.

Sending Food, Supplies, and Money to an Inmate

Sending food, supplies, or money to an inmate detained in the UK prison system is possible, but there are specific procedures you must follow to ensure that everything is sent correctly and according to the rules.

When **sending money**, it is typically deposited into an inmate's personal account, which they use to buy items like toiletries, food from the prison canteen, and other personal necessities. To send money, you can use online payment systems such as **Access Corrections**, which is a service approved by the National Offender Management Service (NOMS). Alternatively, **postal orders** can be used, though this method is slower. Some prisons also accept **bank transfers**, but you'll need to check with the specific prison to see if this is an option. To send money, you'll need the inmate's full name, prisoner number, and the name of the prison they are being held at. Keep in mind that there are **limits on how much money can be sent**, and you may need to pay fees for processing the transaction.

When it comes to sending **food and supplies**, there are stricter regulations in place. While inmates are provided with basic meals and necessary supplies by the prison, family and friends may want to send additional items such as snacks, toiletries, or other personal belongings. Most prisons do not allow homemade or perishable food items to be sent. However, some **approved third-party suppliers** offer pre-packaged food and care packages, which can be sent directly to the inmate. These packages typically contain items like snacks, hygiene products, or books, and they must comply with the prison's strict packaging and security guidelines. If you are unsure whether an item can be sent, it's best to check with the prison directly or use an approved service that adheres to prison regulations.

If you wish to send **clothing**, there are rules as well. Prisons typically allow new clothing to be sent, such as socks or underwear, but they must be **approved beforehand**. Inmates usually wear standard-issue prison clothing, and any extra items will need to meet the prison's approval criteria.

Sending letters is generally allowed, and this is a common way to communicate with someone in prison. However, letters are often subject to inspection for security reasons, and there are rules about the content. You cannot send cash, checks, or anything that could pose a security risk, such as explicit material or items that might be used to smuggle drugs or contraband.

Before sending any money, supplies, or personal items, it is important to familiarize yourself with the specific rules of the prison where the inmate is being held. Each prison has its own set of regulations about what can be sent, how it should be sent, and how it will be processed. Many prisons have guidelines available on their websites, or you can contact the prison directly for more information. It's also important to understand that there may be delays in processing packages, money transfers, or letters due to security checks, and if an item does not comply with the rules, it may be confiscated or returned. Always **double-check the specific regulations of the prison to avoid any complications**, as sending unauthorized items could result in penalties for both the sender and the inmate.

Mail, Phone Calls, and Visitation

In the UK prison system, inmates are allowed to maintain contact with family, friends, and legal representatives through mail, phone calls, and visits, though each is subject to strict regulations.

Inmates can send and receive **mail**, but all correspondence is opened and inspected for security reasons. While letters and postcards are generally allowed, prohibited content, such as drugs or explicit material, will be seized. Outgoing mail is also checked before being sent. Some **legal correspondence** may be sent without being opened, but this must be **clearly marked**. Prisons may impose restrictions on the volume of mail based on the inmate's behavior or security status.

Phone calls are more **restricted**. Inmates must use public phones within the prison and can only call approved contacts, such as family or legal representatives. Calls are often **monitored** and may have **time limits**. The cost of calls is typically deducted from the inmate's personal account, and rates can be higher than regular calls. Emergency calls may be allowed but must be approved by prison staff.

Visitation is allowed but **regulated**. Inmates must have an **approved visitor list**, and all visitors must go through security checks before entering the prison. Visitors may face restrictions based on the inmate's behavior or security level. Typically, inmates can receive visits once or twice a week. **Legal visits** are confidential and **not monitored**, but all other visits are generally conducted through barriers, with some exceptions for private visits for certain inmates.

All forms of communication—mail, phone calls, and visits—are monitored for security purposes, and inmates may face restrictions or penalties based on behavior. High-security inmates may have more limited access to these forms of communication.

Prison Scams

Prison scams are unfortunately common in the UK, with individuals or inmates pretending to be incarcerated and trying to deceive others for financial gain. These scams can take various forms, such as **fake requests for money, false claims of urgent need**, or **deceptive offers to send goods or services to inmates.** In some cases, scammers will call, email, or write to people claiming to be a family member or friend who has been imprisoned and urgently needs money for bail, legal fees, or personal items. There are also scams where individuals pose as lawyers or prison officials, asking for money to help with an inmate's case or to facilitate their release.

The **red flags** that can help identify a scam are fairly consistent. One of the biggest signs is a **sense of urgency**. Scammers often create a false crisis, such as claiming that an inmate urgently needs funds to get out of jail or to avoid legal trouble. They may demand that money be sent immediately, often using high-pressure tactics to prevent you from thinking through the situation. If you receive unsolicited communication from someone claiming to be an inmate or connected to a prison, it's another red flag. Contact that you weren't expecting or that you haven't been informed about should raise suspicions.

Another red flag is if the scammer asks for money through **untraceable methods**, such as gift cards, wire transfers, or pre-paid debit cards. These methods make it difficult to trace the payment and offer little recourse for the victim. Be wary of offers that sound too good to be true, such as promises of a large financial reward for helping an inmate or offers to send packages in exchange for a fee. Additionally, if the contact information provided seems unusual or generic, or if the story being told doesn't add up—like inconsistent details or conflicting information—it's likely a scam.

If you think you're being scammed, the first thing to do is to **stop any transactions or payments immediately**. If you've already sent money, contact your bank or the money transfer service to see if the payment can be reversed. Next, **verify the situation**. Reach out directly to the prison where the inmate is supposedly being held to confirm whether they are there and whether they requested assistance. You can also contact the solicitor or legal team associated with the inmate's case to double-check any claims made.

It's important to **report any suspected scams** as soon as possible. You can report it to **Action Fraud**, the UK's national fraud and cybercrime reporting center. Reporting the scam can help authorities investigate and potentially prevent further fraud. If the scam involved significant amounts of money or caused distress, you should also consider contacting the local police. Letting friends and family know about the scam is also a good idea, as they may be targeted as well.

In addition, make sure to **protect your personal information**. Be cautious about sharing sensitive details such as your financial information, address, or other identifying details, as scammers can use this information for other fraudulent activities. If you receive any communication that seems official, always double-check the contact details with the official prison or legal authorities before responding. Official prison communication is typically formal and will not come through unsolicited channels.

Upon Release

Foreign nationals released from UK prisons may face additional legal obligations and restrictions, particularly related to deportation or immigration status. If a foreign national has been convicted of a serious crime and sentenced to 12 months or more in prison, they are often **subject to deportation**. The Home Office typically makes the decision to deport, and individuals may be detained until they are removed from the UK. If deportation is not immediate, the person might have to report regularly to immigration authorities or comply with other conditions, such as movement restrictions or electronic monitoring. If the foreign national is not deported, they may remain in the UK **under a specific visa**, but this could come with conditions like restrictions on employment, travel, or further reporting to authorities. Additionally, they may be required to **pay any fines, restitution, or compensation** ordered by the court before release.

Foreign nationals should also check for **any exit visa requirements** or travel restrictions imposed by their home country, as some nations may limit the return of citizens with criminal records. In some cases, post-release legal restrictions may include monitoring or limitations on where the person can live or work.

THE ADMINISTRATION OF JUSTICE

THE ADMINISTRATION OF JUSTICE

British Legal System[23]

The British legal system, often referred to as the **English legal system**, is grounded in the principles of **common law**, which has developed over centuries. It primarily applies in **England and Wales**, with separate legal systems in **Scotland** and **Northern Ireland**. Central to the system is the rule of law, which ensures that laws are applied equally to all individuals, and the judiciary is independent from the government.

Unlike many countries, the UK **does not have a single written constitution**. Instead, it relies on **unwritten constitutional principles**, which include **statute law** (laws passed by Parliament), **common law** (decisions made by judges in previous cases), and **conventions** (established practices). The UK also follows the **European Convention on Human Rights** and is bound by certain aspects of **EU law** in areas still applicable after Brexit.

The court structure in the UK is hierarchical, with different courts handling civil and criminal matters. **Magistrates' Courts** deal with less serious criminal cases, preliminary hearings, and some civil matters. More

---

23 https://www.judiciary.uk/about-the-judiciary/our-justice-system/
jud-acc-ind/justice-sys-and-constitution/)

serious crimes, such as murder or fraud, are heard in the **Crown Court**, where a jury typically decides the outcome. The **High Court** deals with complex civil cases and appeals from lower courts, while the **Court of Appeal** hears appeals from both the High Court and the Crown Court. At the top of the system sits the **Supreme Court**, the highest court in the UK, which makes final decisions on significant legal matters, including constitutional issues.

Criminal law in the UK is based on the principle that the state prosecutes offenders for breaking laws that protect society. Crimes are categorized into **indictable offenses** (serious crimes) and **summary offenses** (less serious). The prosecution bears the **burden of proof** in criminal trials, meaning they must prove the defendant's guilt beyond a reasonable doubt. If a case is tried in a **Magistrates' Court**, a panel of lay magistrates or a district judge makes the decision. For more serious crimes, the trial takes place in the **Crown Court**, where a judge oversees the case and a jury renders the verdict.

In **civil law**, the focus is on resolving disputes between individuals or organizations over rights, responsibilities, or wrongs. These can include matters like contracts, property disputes, or personal injury claims. Civil cases are decided on a **balance of probabilities**, meaning one side's case is more likely to be true than the other. The **High Court** handles more complex civil matters, while **County Courts** deal with smaller claims.

Parliament is the primary legislative body in the UK, responsible for creating laws. It consists of two houses: the **House of Commons**, made up of elected Members of Parliament (MPs), and the **House of Lords**, consisting of appointed life peers, hereditary peers, and bishops. Laws are created through a **parliamentary process**, which involves proposing bills, debating them, and voting on them. Once a bill passes both Houses of Parliament, it receives **Royal Assent** before becoming law.

Legal professionals in the UK include **solicitors** and **barristers**. **Solicitors** typically provide legal advice, draft legal documents, and handle routine legal matters, such as contracts and property issues. They may also represent clients in lower courts. **Barristers** specialize in advocacy and represent clients in higher courts, particularly in complex cases or serious criminal matters. Both professions are regulated to ensure ethical conduct and competence.

The **police** are responsible for enforcing the law, investigating crimes, gathering evidence, and making arrests. Police forces in the UK are locally managed but adhere to national guidelines. In more serious cases, specialized units like **MI5** handle national security matters.

The **European Convention on Human Rights** plays a significant role in the UK legal system. The **Human Rights Act 1998** incorporates these rights into domestic law, enabling individuals to bring cases related to human rights violations before UK courts.

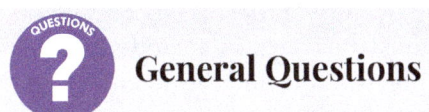 **General Questions**

1. *Will the court treat first-time offenders and tourists with more leniency?* In the UK, the court may take into consideration whether the defendant is a first-time offender, but this does not automatically result in leniency. For first-time offenders, the court may opt for a less severe sentence, especially if the crime is minor and the individual shows remorse. However, the nature of the offense, any mitigating circumstances, and the defendant's background are also important factors in sentencing. For tourists, the fact that they are not residents of the UK may be considered during sentencing, particularly if the crime involves factors like cultural misunderstanding. However, the court generally treats all offenders based on the seriousness of the crime and applicable sentencing guidelines, regardless of whether they are a first-time offender or a tourist.

2. *If I am charged with a crime, which court is likely to hear my case?* In the UK, the court that hears your case depends on how serious the crime is. Minor offenses, like driving violations or shoplifting, are usually handled by a Magistrates' Court. More serious crimes, such as robbery or murder, go to a Crown Court, which involves a judge and jury. Some crimes, called "either-way offenses" like theft, can be heard in either court depending on the case details and sometimes the defendant's choice. Regardless, your first appearance will almost always be at a Magistrates' Court, which then decides whether the case stays there or moves to the Crown Court.

3. *What is the standard of proof in a criminal case in the UK?* In the UK, the standard of proof in a criminal case is "beyond a reasonable doubt." This means that the prosecution must prove the defendant's guilt to such a degree that there is no reasonable doubt in the minds of the judge or jury. If there is any reasonable doubt about the defendant's guilt, they must be acquitted. The burden of proof lies with the prosecution, and the defense does not have to prove the defendant's innocence.

 **Takeaways**

- The UK operates under common law with separate legal systems for England and Wales, Scotland, and Northern Ireland. It lacks a written constitution, relying on statutes, common law, and conventions. The court system is hierarchical, with the Supreme Court at the top.

- In criminal cases, the **prosecution must prove guilt beyond a reasonable doubt.** In civil cases, the standard is the balance of probabilities. Minor crimes are handled by Magistrates' Courts, while more serious cases go to the Crown Court.

- Courts may show leniency to first-time offenders, especially for minor crimes, and consider cultural misunderstandings for tourists.

However, sentencing depends on the offense's severity and other factors like remorse.

- In the UK, solicitors handle legal advice and lower court cases, while barristers specialize in advocacy in higher courts. The police enforce laws, and the Human Rights Act 1998 allows human rights cases to be heard in UK courts.

CRIME VICTIM ASSISTANCE

- Overview
- What to Do If You Are the Victim of a Crime
- Common Tourist Scams in the UK
- Sexual Assault
- Consular Assistance
- General Questions

CRIME VICTIM ASSISTANCE

Overview

In the UK, crime victims have access to a wide range of assistance and support to help them cope with the emotional, financial, and legal impacts of a crime. One of the main resources is **Victim Support**, a charity that provides free and confidential help to anyone affected by crime. Victim Support offers emotional support, practical advice, and guidance on navigating the criminal justice system, as well as assistance with compensation claims.[24]

For those who have suffered from violent crimes, the **Criminal Injuries Compensation Authority** (**CICA**) provides financial compensation to help cover medical costs, lost wages, and other expenses related to the crime. The **National Victim Helpline** (0808 168 9111) is another valuable resource, offering 24/7 advice and information to victims about their rights, available support services, and how the criminal justice system works.

Specialized services are available for victims of specific crimes. **Refuge** and **Rape Crisis** provide support to victims of domestic violence and sexual assault, respectively. **The LGBT Foundation** offers targeted help for LGBT victims of crime, while services like **Stop Hate UK** provide support for victims of hate crimes. Victims may also be offered the

---

24 https://www.victimsupport.org.uk/

opportunity to take part in **restorative justice programs**, where they can meet the offender (under safe conditions) to discuss the impact of the crime and possibly contribute to the offender's rehabilitation.

For legal support, victims may be eligible for **legal aid**, especially when pursuing compensation claims or seeking assistance with legal matters related to the crime. Families of victims also receive support from charities like **Families Against Murder and Suicide** (**FAMS**), which helps relatives deal with grief, legal proceedings, and emotional challenges after a violent crime.

These resources ensure that crime victims in the UK have access to the support they need for recovery, justice, and understanding their rights.

What to Do If You Are the Victim of a Crime

If you are a victim of a crime in the UK, the first thing you should do is ensure your immediate safety. If you're in danger, call **999** for emergency services. If the situation is less urgent but still requires police attention, you can call **101** or visit your local police station. If you are unable to visit in person, you can report the crime online or contact **Crimestoppers** anonymously.

Once you're safe, it's important to **report the crime to the police.** Provide as much detail as possible, including descriptions of the suspect(s), the crime itself, and any evidence you might have. If there is physical evidence related to the crime, try to preserve it. For instance, if you've been assaulted or experienced sexual violence, avoid washing, changing clothes, or cleaning up, as this could destroy important evidence.

If you've been physically injured, **seek medical attention** right away. You can visit your GP, go to a walk-in center, or head to the emergency department, depending on the severity of the injury. For sexual assault victims, it's recommended to visit a **Sexual Assault Referral Centre** (**SARC**), which provides confidential medical care, forensic examination, and support.

After reporting the crime, you can access support through **Victim Support**, a charity that offers free and confidential services for all crime victims. They can help with emotional support, guide you through the legal process, and inform you of your rights. If necessary, you can also **consult a solicitor**, who can offer legal advice, especially if you plan to seek compensation or are involved in a criminal case. Depending on the crime, you may be eligible for compensation through the **Criminal Injuries Compensation Authority** (**CICA**).

If you feel comfortable, you can also explore restorative justice programs, which allow victims to meet with offenders in a controlled environment to discuss the crime's impact. This is voluntary and may be helpful for some victims in their healing process. Additionally, specialized support services, such as **Rape Crisis** for sexual violence or **Refuge** for domestic abuse, can provide tailored help.

Finally, stay in contact with the police and victim support services for updates on your case and keep records of any correspondence, legal proceedings, or counseling sessions. This will help you remain informed and supported throughout the process.

Common Tourist Scams in the UK[25]

Tourists in the UK, particularly in major cities like London, can be targeted by a variety of scams. These scams often prey on people who are unfamiliar with the area or distracted by their travel plans.

One of the most common scams involves **overcharging by taxi drivers** or **fake taxis**. While black cabs in London are reliable, tourists might be approached by unlicensed taxis or drivers offering deals. These drivers may charge exorbitant fares or take longer routes. Always use licensed taxi services or apps like Uber and confirm the fare before getting in.

---

25 https://www.godigit.com/intenational-travel-insurance/tourist-scams/tourist-scams-in-uk

Another frequent scam targets tourists near popular attractions, such as **theft** or **pickpocketing**. Thieves often work in groups, distracting their victims with a variety of tactics, including asking for directions or pretending to be street performers. To avoid falling victim, stay vigilant in crowded areas, keep valuables close, and use money belts or neck pouches.

Fake charity collectors are also a common scam targeting tourists. Fraudsters approach individuals in busy areas, claiming to be collecting donations for a charity, but they pocket the money themselves. Be cautious of people approaching you in tourist spots and always verify charity collections by looking for official identification or checking the charity's legitimacy online.

Accommodation scams are also on the rise, especially for those booking lodging through unverified websites or social media platforms. These scammers may offer fake rental properties and ask for deposits or payment upfront. Always book through trusted platforms, read reviews, and confirm details before making payments.

Overpriced or fake tickets to attractions, tours, or transportation are common scams in areas with many tourists. Scammers may offer tickets to sold-out events at inflated prices or sell fake tickets that are invalid. Only purchase tickets from official outlets or trusted vendors.

To avoid these scams, always be cautious when approached by strangers and avoid sharing personal information. Use official services, double-check prices and bookings, and keep your belongings secure. If something feels off, trust your instincts, and don't hesitate to report suspicious behavior to local authorities.

Sexual Assault

If you have been the victim of sexual assault in the UK, it's important to prioritize your immediate safety and well-being. The first step is to ensure you are in a **safe location**. If you are in immediate danger or need urgent help, call **999** for emergency services. If possible, remove yourself from the situation and seek a trusted friend or family member for support. If you're alone, you may consider going to a public area or somewhere familiar where you feel safe.

It's important to report the assault as soon as you feel able. You can report the incident to the police by calling **101** or visiting your local police station. You can also report a sexual assault anonymously through **Crimestoppers**. Reporting the crime can help prevent further assaults and may provide important support for your recovery.

If you wish to preserve evidence, avoid washing, changing clothes, or cleaning yourself up, as this can destroy crucial evidence. If you are unsure, it's a good idea to go directly to a **Sexual Assault Referral Centre** (**SARC**), which offers free and confidential medical care, forensic examinations, and emotional support. These centers provide specialized services and can guide you through the process of reporting the crime and preserving evidence, all while maintaining your privacy.

As a victim of sexual assault, you have several important rights. You are entitled to be treated with dignity, respect, and confidentiality throughout the legal and medical process. You also have the right to access **Victim Support**, a charity that offers free, confidential services to help you through the criminal justice process. If you choose to report the assault, you will also have the right to legal representation and the option to seek **Criminal Injuries Compensation** through the **Criminal Injuries Compensation Authority** (**CICA**) if the assault resulted in physical or psychological harm.

If you decide not to report the assault immediately or at all, it's still important to seek emotional and psychological support. Many sexual assault survivors benefit from counseling, therapy, or talking to a trained professional. Organizations like **Rape Crisis UK** provide confidential support and can help you make informed decisions about next steps.

For **safety recommendations**, avoid walking alone late at night in poorly lit areas and consider using transport services like licensed taxis or rideshare apps to get home safely. It's also helpful to let someone know your whereabouts when going out, especially if you're in an unfamiliar area. Trust your instincts and if something feels unsafe, remove yourself from the situation as quickly as possible.

Finally, while healing from a sexual assault can be a long and difficult process, remember that you are not alone. There are multiple organizations and professionals dedicated to supporting survivors, and accessing help is an important part of recovery.

Consular Assistance

If you're a foreign national in the UK and need assistance, your embassy or consulate can provide a range of **crucial services**. While they cannot offer legal advice, they can help you find a local lawyer, especially if you face criminal charges or are arrested. In case of lost documents, they can issue emergency travel documents to help you return home. If you're in financial difficulty, they can assist in facilitating funds from family or friends back home, but they don't provide direct financial aid themselves.

Embassies also support victims of crime by helping you contact local authorities, guiding you through the legal process, and providing resources for legal, psychological, or emotional support. In health-related emergencies, they can help you find local medical services but cannot offer medical treatment. If you face a personal crisis, such as illness or the death of a family member, consulates can assist with repatriating remains or helping you return home.

However, there are **limits to consular assistance**. They cannot provide legal representation, intervene in the legal process, nor can they prevent or alter legal outcomes. They can't offer loans for personal expenses, legal fees, or medical bills, and they cannot override UK laws or immigration procedures. Consular services may also be limited outside regular office hours, so it's important to be aware of their specific guidelines for assistance.

 **General Questions**

1. *If I am a victim of a crime, can I legally be compensated?* **Yes.** If you're a victim of crime in the UK, you may be eligible for compensation. The Criminal Injuries Compensation Scheme (CICS) provides compensation for those injured or traumatized by violent crime, but you must report the crime to the police and cooperate with the investigation. You may also pursue compensation through civil court for personal injury claims if the crime involved negligence, though this depends on the offender's ability to pay. However, the CICS has a time limit for claims, and it doesn't cover property loss or theft.

2. *If a family member falls victim to homicide, can I bring the body back to my home country?* **Yes.** If a family member is a homicide victim in the UK, you can arrange to bring their body back to your home country. After the police investigation and post-mortem, the coroner must release the body. A funeral director can assist with the necessary paperwork, permits, embalming, and transport. You may need to provide documents such as proof of identity and relationship. Your embassy can offer guidance, but repatriation costs are generally the family's responsibility.

3. *3. What legal protections are available for victims of stalking in the UK?* In the UK, victims of stalking are protected under the **Protection from Harassment Act 1997** and the **Stalking Protection Act 2019**. Stalking offenses can lead to criminal charges, including harassment, and perpetrators can face a restraining order. The **Stalking Protection Orders** (SPOs) can be issued by the court to impose conditions on the stalker, such as preventing them from contacting the victim or coming near their home. Victims can also seek support through **Victim Support** and report incidents to the police, who can investigate and provide immediate protection.

POLICE

CHAPTER 15

POLICE

Overview[26]

The UK does not have a federal police system like some other countries. Instead, the country's police forces are organized at the local level, with each force responsible for a specific geographical area. These forces operate across three main categories: **national**, **regional**, and **local** police.

The largest and most well-known force is the **Metropolitan Police Service** (**MPS**), which covers Greater London (excluding the City of London). In addition, there are **constabularies** in other areas of England and Wales, as well as **police forces** in Scotland and Northern Ireland. Scotland has a single national force, **Police Scotland**, while Northern Ireland's police service is **Police Service of Northern Ireland** (**PSNI**).

Each police force has its own responsibilities:

- **Local police** (constabularies) handle general law enforcement duties such as responding to crimes, patrolling neighborhoods, and engaging with the community.

---

26 https://en.wikipedia.org/wiki/
    Law_enforcement_in_the_United_Kingdom

- **National police** forces, like the **National Crime Agency (NCA)**, focus on tackling serious crime, organized crime, cybercrime, and national security issues.

- **Specialist units** exist for specific issues like counterterrorism (e.g., **Counter Terrorism Policing**), and some regions have **traffic police** or **border enforcement** services.

As of recent estimates, the UK has around **160,000 police officers**, including both front-line officers and support staff across various forces. The total number fluctuates but is generally divided among more than 40 different police forces. While the police force in the UK is generally regarded as being **adequately staffed** for day-to-day responsibilities, concerns have been raised in recent years about increased pressure on resources, particularly due to cuts in funding and rising demand, especially in areas like counterterrorism, cybercrime, and domestic violence. There has been an emphasis on increasing officer numbers and improving response times in light of these challenges, but the adequacy of staffing can vary by region and the nature of the crimes being tackled..

Police Response

The **UK police forces** are responsible for several key functions that ensure public safety and maintain order. Their primary functions include **crime prevention, investigation, enforcement of laws**, and **maintaining public order**. They handle a wide range of responsibilities, from responding to emergency calls and investigating crimes (such as theft, assault, and murder) to managing public events and ensuring road safety. The police also engage in community outreach and education programs aimed at preventing crime and building trust with the public. Another important function is **counterterrorism**, where special units like Counter Terrorism Policing focus on protecting the UK from terrorist threats.

Despite these essential functions, the UK police face **several challenges**. One significant issue is **funding cuts**, which have led to reductions in staffing levels and resources in some areas. This has been exacerbated by **increased demand**, especially in tackling complex crimes like cybercrime, domestic violence, and child exploitation. Another challenge is **public trust** and **accountability**, particularly in the wake of high-profile incidents of police misconduct or racial bias. There are also concerns about how police are handling new types of crime, such as **online harassment** and **terrorist radicalization.**

In terms of ongoing reforms, there has been a push toward **increasing diversity** within the police force and improving **community policing** to rebuild trust. The government has also focused on reforming the way **mental health** is handled by police, often advocating for better training for officers to deal with vulnerable individuals and diverting them from the criminal justice system when appropriate. Additionally, the **National Crime Agency** (**NCA**) has been playing an increasingly important role in combating serious and organized crime, while the police have been expanding their **use of technology**, such as facial recognition and AI, to enhance crime prevention and detection.

Police and Community Relations

The overall image and perception of the police in the UK are **varied**, with public opinion shaped by factors like location, specific events, and interactions with law enforcement. In general, many people appreciate the role of the police in maintaining public safety and law and order. In smaller communities and rural areas, local police are often seen as approachable and effective in resolving issues, and residents typically feel a sense of security.

However, in urban areas and among certain minority groups, the police face more criticism. Concerns around racial profiling, the use of force, and transparency have led to tension between law enforcement and some communities. Certain groups, especially Black and ethnic minority communities, have expressed frustration over practices like stop-and-search, which they argue disproportionately target them. Public confidence in the police has been further challenged by concerns about accountability and misconduct.

While the police remain crucial to maintaining order, the image of law enforcement in the UK is undergoing scrutiny, with growing calls for **reform, better training**, and **improved community engagement**. Public opinion is evolving, and efforts are underway to rebuild trust through increased transparency, better oversight, and stronger ties between the police and local communities.

Police Use of Force

Police use of force is an issue in the UK, though it is less prevalent and typically less severe compared to some other countries, such as the United States. However, there have been several high-profile incidents and concerns raised about excessive use of force, particularly in relation to **racial profiling, vulnerable individuals**, and **police accountability**.

While the majority of interactions between police and the public do not involve the use of force, certain instances have sparked significant public debate. These include cases where force may have been deemed excessive or disproportionate to the situation, such as **police shootings, violent arrests**, or the use of force at public protests.

Some high-profile cases that have drawn attention to the issue include the **death of Chris Kaba** in 2022, where a Black man was shot and killed by an armed officer during a car chase. This case raised questions about the use of lethal force in non-terror-related incidents and led to calls for greater transparency and accountability in police actions. For more on this case, see the Law of the Land True Story below. Another prominent case was the **Sarah Everard tragedy**, where a police officer was convicted of a violent crime, leading to broader concerns about the treatment of women by the police and the misuse of power within law enforcement.

The **Independent Office for Police Conduct (IOPC)** plays a role in investigating complaints and allegations of police misconduct, but critics argue that oversight and accountability mechanisms are sometimes insufficient, especially in cases of **racial discrimination** or **disproportionate use** of force against minority communities.

In response, there have been calls for better police training, greater oversight, and reforms in how the police manage situations involving vulnerable individuals or protests. While there is no widespread perception that the UK police force is overly violent, these cases have highlighted significant concerns regarding police conduct and the need for ongoing reforms in how force is applied in policing.

Law of the Land True Story[27]

The case of Chris Kaba, a 24-year-old man shot and killed by police officer Martyn Blake in September 2022, has sparked significant controversy in the UK. Kaba, who was unarmed, was shot in the head during a police vehicle stop in South London after attempting to flee when surrounded by officers. Blake, who claimed he acted out of fear for his colleagues' safety, was acquitted of murder in October 2024. The acquittal has led to public outrage, with Kaba's family and supporters describing the decision as a "failure" for justice, highlighting the broader issue of police accountability, especially in cases involving the use of force.

This case is directly related to ongoing concerns about unauthorized and excessive use of police force in the UK, particularly in incidents involving racial dynamics. The public response, including protests and calls for justice, underscores a deep mistrust of the legal system's ability to hold police officers accountable. Critics argue that this case represents the broader issue of police impunity, where officers may face little to no consequences for lethal actions taken in the line of duty. Despite the jury's decision, campaigners and activists have vowed to continue the fight for greater police accountability, racial equality, and reform of the justice system to prevent such cases from happening in the future. The ongoing debate about police violence, particularly against minority communities, is central to discussions about reform and the need for better oversight of law enforcement practices in the UK.

---

27 https://www.bbc.com/news/articles/c17lk592ygdo

HOW TO GET LEGAL HELP IN THE UK

- Available Resources
- Legal Aid
- Foreign Embassies in the UK

HOW TO GET LEGAL HELP IN THE UK

Available Resources

If you find yourself in legal trouble while in the UK, there are several steps and resources that can help you navigate the situation. First, if you are facing an emergency or need to report a crime, the police can be contacted by dialing **999** for urgent matters or **101** for non-urgent situations. In cases where you are arrested or detained, it's important to know that the police are required to inform you of your rights, including the right to remain silent and the right to legal representation.

If you're a foreign national, your embassy or consulate can provide crucial assistance. While the embassy or consulate can provide you with legal resources, including a list of local solicitors and barristers, they themselves cannot provide legal representation. For legal representation, contacting an experienced solicitor is essential. Solicitors in the UK can offer legal advice, represent you in court, and assist with various legal proceedings. You can find a solicitor through online directories, law firms, or by asking your embassy for a list of reputable lawyers. The **Law Society**[28], for example, has a "Find a Solicitor" service to help you locate professionals in your area. If you cannot afford to hire a solicitor, you may be eligible for **legal aid**, a government service that covers

---

28   https://www.lawsociety.org.uk

legal costs for individuals with limited financial means. In addition, the **Citizens Advice Bureau (CAB)**[29] offers free, impartial advice on a wide range of legal matters. Whether you're unsure about your rights or need assistance with a particular case, the CAB can point you in the right direction and help you understand your options.

If the situation involves potential police misconduct, the **Independent Office for Police Conduct (IOPC)** investigates complaints against the police. They can help you if you believe you've been treated unfairly or subjected to mistreatment by law enforcement officers. They can be reached through their website at **https://www.policeconduct.gov.uk.**

By reaching out to these resources, you can ensure that you receive the legal assistance and support needed to address any legal issues you may face while in the UK.

Legal Aid[30]

In the UK, legal aid is available to certain individuals who meet specific criteria, but it generally applies to residents or those with a strong connection to the country. **Foreign visitors may be eligible for legal aid**, though this is more limited. Legal aid is typically available for cases where a person is facing serious charges or needs assistance with complex legal matters, like criminal defense or family law.

The eligibility for legal aid depends on factors like the individual's income, assets, and the nature of the case. For foreign visitors, eligibility may be limited unless they are **in the UK lawfully** and **have a connection to the country**, such as being in the process of seeking asylum or having a valid visa. The process typically involves an application where the applicant's financial situation is assessed, and whether the case is considered serious enough to merit legal aid.

---

29 https://www.citizensadvice.org.uk/

30 https://www.nrpfnetwork.org.uk/information-and-resources/
    rights-and-entitlements/legal-aid

Legal aid can cover various costs, including legal representation in court, solicitor fees, and other legal expenses. It can also cover some civil cases, such as housing or immigration issues, if the person meets the financial eligibility requirements. However, not all cases are eligible, and legal aid is subject to availability, with priority given to more serious legal issues.

Foreign Embassies in the UK

Foreign embassies and consulates in the UK play a crucial role in supporting and protecting their citizens abroad. They offer a range of services, including consular assistance, issuing passports, providing legal and emergency support, assisting with arrests or detentions, and facilitating travel documents for nationals. They also work on diplomatic and economic relations between their home country and the UK.

Embassies are predominantly located in the capital city, **London**, while **consulates** can be found in other major cities such as **Edinburgh**, **Manchester**, or **Birmingham**. Embassies typically handle more formal and political matters, while consulates are primarily focused on assisting citizens and managing consular services, such as Passport Services, Notarization and Legal Assistance, Emergency Assistance, Arrest and Detention Assistance, Travel Documentation, Financial Assistance, Victim Support, and Consular Protection.

For U.S. nationals, the **U.S. Embassy** in London, located at 33 Nine Elms Lane, is the primary diplomatic mission. There are also U.S. consulates in other cities such as Belfast, Edinburgh, and in Northern Ireland, where Americans can access consular services.

 To find other embassies and consulates from different countries in the UK, you can visit **https://www.gov.uk/ government/publications/foreign-embassies-in-the-uk**, which provides comprehensive links to embassies and consulates of various countries in the United Kingdom.

MEDICAL FACILITIES & HOSPITALS

MEDICAL FACILITIES & HOSPITALS

Overview[31]

The healthcare system in the United Kingdom is primarily structured around the **National Health Service (NHS)**, which provides most health services for free at the point of use, funded through taxation. It is **one of the largest publicly funded health services in the world**, and its design aims to ensure universal access to healthcare for all residents of the UK, regardless of income or status.

Healthcare in the UK operates through a system of publicly funded services, with primary care (GP services) at the forefront. The healthcare system is decentralized, with different countries in the UK (England, Scotland, Wales, and Northern Ireland) managing their healthcare services **independently**, although all of them are founded on the NHS principles. **General Practitioners** (GPs) are typically the first point of contact for most patients, offering general medical care, prescribing medication, and referring patients to specialists. Secondary care involves **specialists**, such as cardiologists or dermatologists, who patients are referred to by their GP, while tertiary care involves specialized treatments and surgeries often provided by **hospitals**.

---

31 https://eurohealthobservatory.who.int/publications/i/
    united-kingdom-health-system-summary

Emergency services are available through **Accident & Emergency** (**A&E**) departments, and ambulance services are available 24/7 for critical emergencies. Mental health services are also provided by the NHS, ranging from outpatient counseling to inpatient psychiatric care. The NHS is primarily delivered through **NHS Trusts**, which are organizations responsible for running hospitals, clinics, and other care services, some of which are specialized, such as mental health or community care trusts.

The accessibility of healthcare in the UK is generally considered to be good, though there are challenges. The system aims to make healthcare services **available to everyone**, but accessibility can vary based on factors such as geographic location, wait times, and GP access. People in **rural or remote areas** might face **longer waiting times** or **difficulty accessing specialized care**, though the NHS has worked to address this through telemedicine and mobile healthcare services. Wait times, especially for non-emergency procedures, are often a source of criticism, with patients facing long waiting lists for elective surgeries or specialist referrals, particularly in England, which has a higher population density compared to other parts of the UK. Access to GPs can also be difficult in high-demand areas, although online consultations and telephone appointments have been increasingly utilized to improve access. However, these digital solutions can create barriers for people without reliable internet access or digital literacy.

The **quality of healthcare** in the UK **varies by region**, but overall, the NHS delivers high-quality care in many areas, especially preventive care and emergency services. The NHS places significant **emphasis on prevention, including immunizations, cancer screenings**, and **public health campaigns**. Emergency care is generally fast and efficient, with the ambulance services being well-regarded, although ambulance response times have been under pressure in recent years due to workforce shortages and increased demand. Clinical outcomes, such as life expectancy, maternal and child health, and cancer survival rates, are generally strong and on par with other developed nations. However, chronic conditions like diabetes and cardiovascular diseases remain a challenge. The quality of care can sometimes be affected by workforce shortages in areas such as nursing, mental health, and primary care, which can lead to longer wait times, reduced patient satisfaction, or even safety concerns.

The **affordability of medical services** in the UK is one of the NHS's core strengths, as most services are **free at the point of use**. The system is funded through general taxation, which means that **residents do not face out-of-pocket costs for most services**, including GP consultations, hospital stays, surgeries, and emergency care. However, there are some areas where patients may need to pay. **Prescription charges apply in England**, though exemptions exist for children, the elderly, and people with certain conditions. Prescription charges are **not levied in Scotland, Wales, or Northern Ireland. Dental** and **optometry services** are **not fully covered** by the NHS. While NHS dental care is subsidized, patients often pay a portion of the cost, and private dental care can be expensive. Eye tests are free for some groups, but glasses and contact lenses generally require payment. Some individuals opt for **private healthcare**, which offers faster access to specialists and elective surgeries, but it comes at an additional personal cost.

Despite the many strengths of the NHS, the system faces **several challenges. Funding pressures** are significant, particularly with the rising demands of an aging population and increasing chronic health conditions. The system needs to adapt to meet these rising demands while maintaining the quality of care. **Staffing shortages**, especially in areas like nursing, primary care, and emergency services, are also a concern, with high levels of burnout and difficulty in recruitment, particularly following the impacts of Brexit. Additionally, **delays in treatment**, such as long waiting times for elective procedures or specialist consultations, have been a persistent issue, exacerbated by the COVID-19 pandemic. Although the NHS is universal, **health inequalities persist**, particularly among lower socioeconomic groups and certain ethnic communities, who may face barriers to accessing care and tend to have poorer health outcomes.

Here are a few of the most important emergency numbers in the UK:

- **Emergency services (police, fire, ambulance):** 999
- **Alternative to 999, works across the EU:** 112
- **NHS non-emergency medical advice:** 111
- **Non-emergency police contact:** 101

- **Childline (support for children and young people):** 0800 1111
- **Samaritans (emotional support, 24/7):** 116 123
- **National Domestic Violence Helpline (24/7):** 0800 055 5112

Visitors' Access to Healthcare in the UK[32]

Visitors to the UK can access healthcare, but the process depends on their status and the type of treatment they need. While the UK's National Health Service (NHS) primarily serves residents, **emergency care, including services at Accident & Emergency (A&E) departments and ambulance services, is free for visitors**. However, follow-up care or non-emergency treatment may require payment, unless the visitor is from a country with a **reciprocal healthcare agreement** with the UK. After Brexit, the **Global Health Insurance Card (GHIC)** replaced the European Health Insurance Card (EHIC) for EU visitors, offering similar coverage.

For primary care, such as **GP visits,** visitors are typically required to pay unless they have insurance or reciprocal coverage. Private GPs and specialists are available but can be costly. Visitors are strongly advised to have **travel insurance** to cover medical expenses, as out-of-pocket payments for NHS care can be expensive, particularly for hospital stays or surgeries.

Language barriers pose another significant challenge for visitors seeking medical help. Many visitors may struggle to communicate with healthcare providers, particularly if they are not fluent in English. Although the NHS offers **interpretation services**, their availability and quality vary depending on location, and visitors may need to request them in advance. Private healthcare providers may offer better access to multilingual services, but these typically come at a higher cost. Visitors can also rely on translation apps, but they may not always be reliable in medical settings, where precision is crucial.

---

32 https://www.nhs.uk/nhs-services/visiting-or-moving-to-england/
how-to-access-nhs-services-in-england-if-you-are-visiting-from-abroad/

In addition to communication issues, **cultural differences** can complicate healthcare experiences. Visitors from different cultural backgrounds may have varying expectations of healthcare, leading to potential misunderstandings or discomfort. Overall, visitors to the UK need to plan ahead by securing travel insurance and considering potential language and cultural barriers when accessing healthcare services.

The UK's Hospitals

The UK has a well-established healthcare system primarily through the National Health Service (NHS), which provides public healthcare across hospitals, clinics, and other healthcare facilities. There are approximately **1,250 hospitals** across the UK, with about **1,000 in England** alone. NHS hospitals employ around **1.3 million staff**, including doctors, nurses, and other healthcare professionals. In addition, there are about **200 private hospitals** scattered across the country, mainly in larger cities.

Hospitals are concentrated in **urban areas**, especially in **London**, **Manchester**, **Birmingham**, and **Edinburgh**. The major metropolitan areas tend to have the highest number of hospitals due to the population density and the concentration of specialist services. For instance, **London** has a large number of world-renowned hospitals and medical centers, making it a hub for medical care in the UK. Other cities with significant hospital clusters include **Bristol**, **Leeds**, and **Glasgow**. While urban centers have the most healthcare facilities, rural areas and smaller towns often have fewer hospitals, with some depending on smaller community hospitals or regional medical centers. However, the NHS aims to ensure that most populations are within reasonable reach of medical care, with emergency services often available even in remote or rural locations through regional hubs and air ambulance support.

International visitors can access medical services at both **NHS hospitals** and **private hospitals**, but typically, NHS care is free only for residents or those from countries with reciprocal healthcare agreements. Visitors from countries without agreements are usually required to pay for treatment.

Hospitals in major cities, particularly London, are well-equipped to cater to international patients. Some hospitals have dedicated services for international visitors, with multilingual staff and international patient liaison teams. Hospitals like **The London Clinic** and **The Portland Hospital** are known for offering specialized services to international visitors, often including VIP treatment, faster access, and private consultations.

There are also **medical tourism services** in the UK, where international patients can access world-class care, particularly in fields like **cosmetic surgery, fertility treatments, orthopedic surgery,** and **cancer care.** Many private hospitals, including **The Harley Street Clinic** in London, are popular with overseas patients seeking specialized medical care.

There is **no specific "American hospital"** in the UK in the sense of a hospital solely operated by an American entity. However, **American-style hospitals** with a focus on high-quality private care do exist. Many of these private facilities offer services familiar to American patients, including a more personalized approach to healthcare, quicker access to treatment, and the option for English-speaking staff. Notable examples include:

- **The American Hospital (London):** This is not an actual hospital but rather a **private healthcare provider** that caters specifically to American expatriates and international visitors in London. The clinic provides medical services and consultations with American-trained doctors.

- **The Wellington Hospital (London):** Part of the **HCA Healthcare UK network**, this private healthcare group has with a strong American connection. HCA Healthcare is a large American for-profit healthcare organization, and its UK hospitals are known for their high standards of care.

While these hospitals may provide a more "American" feel in terms of customer service and healthcare delivery, they are not operated as part of a network of American-owned hospitals in the UK. Nonetheless, their services are tailored to meet the needs of international patients, particularly those from the US.

General Questions

1. *What should you do if you feel unwell/sick in the UK?* If you feel unwell or sick in the UK, your first step is to assess the severity of your symptoms to determine the right care. For minor ailments like a cold or stomach upset, a **pharmacy** is often the best first stop, as pharmacists are trained to offer advice and over-the-counter remedies. If the issue requires more medical attention, visiting a **GP** is the next option. GPs serve as the primary healthcare providers in the UK, and you can book an appointment with one, although there may be fees for non-residents or those without insurance coverage. Many GPs also offer online consultations, which is convenient for visitors. For more urgent, but non-life-threatening conditions, **Urgent Care Centres** are available and can treat issues such as high fever, severe pain, or deep cuts. These centers operate outside of regular GP hours and are typically found in larger cities. In the case of a serious emergency, such as chest pain or breathing difficulties, you should visit the **Accident & Emergency** (**A&E**) department of a hospital, which is open 24/7 and offers free treatment for life-threatening conditions. However, follow-up care or non-emergency treatments may come with a charge for visitors.

2. *What type of health insurance should visitors have when traveling to the UK to ensure coverage for medical emergencies, and does the European Health Insurance Card (EHIC) still apply post-Brexit?* If you're traveling to the UK, it's crucial to have **travel insurance** that covers medical emergencies, as the National Health Service (NHS) typically charges for services for non-residents. Post-Brexit, **EU visitors** should use the **Global Health Insurance Card** (**GHIC**) for limited NHS access, but non-EU visitors need comprehensive insurance to avoid high medical costs.

3. *What should visitors do if they require urgent medical care but do not have NHS coverage or travel insurance, and how much could treatment potentially cost?* If you require urgent medical care without NHS coverage or insurance, you can still receive treatment at **Accident & Emergency (A&E)** for life-threatening conditions. However, follow-up care or non-emergency treatment will incur significant costs, potentially running into thousands of pounds (U.S. dollars) for services like surgery or hospital stays. It's recommended to have **travel insurance** to cover these expenses.

4. *Are there specialized healthcare services or medical evacuation options for visitors in the UK, particularly for those who may need to be transported back to their home country for treatment?* For travelers requiring medical evacuation, private healthcare providers and services like **International SOS** or **Air Ambulance Worldwide** offer medical repatriation. These services can arrange transportation to a hospital in your home country, often facilitated through your travel insurance, and are available in major cities like London and Manchester.

Insurance Guidance[33]

Foreign insurance plans are **generally accepted** in the UK, but the level of coverage depends on the provider and the type of care required. **Travel insurance** is often the best option for visitors, as it can cover emergency medical treatment, hospital stays, and repatriation. Some international health insurance plans may also be accepted at private healthcare facilities. However, for NHS services, non-residents typically need to pay unless they are from a country with a reciprocal healthcare agreement or they have the **Global Health Insurance Card (GHIC)** for EU citizens.

The cost of medical services in the UK varies depending on the type of care. A visit to the **Accident & Emergency (A&E)** department is **free**

---

33 https://www.internations.org/costa-rica-expats/guide/healthcare

for life-threatening emergencies, but for **non-urgent cases**, you may have to pay up to **£120** (about US$155) **or more** for an A&E consultation. **GP visits** can cost between **£30-£60** (about US$39-$77) if you're not registered with the NHS. **Private consultations** with a specialist or doctor can range from **£100 to £250** (about US$129-$323), depending on the complexity of the treatment. Private hospital stays and surgeries can cost thousands of pounds (US dollars), making travel insurance essential for covering these potential expenses.

For payment, if you are using **NHS services**, residents are typically covered by taxes, but **visitors will be required to pay unless covered by insurance or an international agreement**. In **private healthcare**, you will need to **pay upfront** for services unless your travel insurance covers the costs. Payments can typically be made via **credit card, debit card,** or **cash,** and some private clinics may require advance payment for treatments. If you have insurance, you may need to submit claims afterward for reimbursement, depending on the policy.

DRIVING IN THE UK

DRIVING IN THE UK

Overview

Driving in the UK offers a generally **well-organized experience**, thanks to its **well-maintained road infrastructure**. Major highways and motorways like the M1 and M25 are in good condition, with clear signage and regular maintenance, making long-distance driving smooth. Urban roads are also well-kept, though they can be narrow, especially in older areas with cobblestone streets. In rural areas, roads are quieter but may not be as well-maintained, especially in remote locations.

A key feature of UK roads is the **prevalence of roundabouts**, which help with traffic flow but may be tricky for unfamiliar drivers, especially in busy areas. At roundabouts, vehicles already on the roundabout have priority, and drivers should signal left when exiting. Flashing headlights is often used to signal intentions, such as letting another driver go ahead, but it's not for overtaking. Using indicators well in advance is crucial, particularly on roundabouts and motorways, as failure to signal can result in fines.

Signage is **clear and frequent**, with speed limits and directions well-marked. However, **traffic congestion** is a **significant issue** in cities like London, where rush-hour delays are common, and parking can be expensive and hard to find. **Safety** is a **top priority**, with strict laws on seat belts, mobile phones, and drink driving, and speed cameras monitoring major routes. Weather conditions, especially rain and fog, can affect driving, with slippery roads and reduced visibility being common in winter months.

Driving in the UK also means adjusting to **driving on the left side** of the road. While UK drivers tend to be courteous and follow road safety rules, cyclists are also given attention with dedicated bike lanes in many cities. Parking regulations are strict, with double yellow lines indicating no parking at any time, and single yellow lines meaning parking is restricted during certain hours. At pedestrian crossings, particularly zebra crossings, pedestrians have the right of way.

When driving in the UK as a foreign driver, there are **specific documentation** and **insurance requirements** to keep in mind. First, you must possess a **valid driving license**. If your license is not in English, it's advisable to carry an **International Driving Permit** (IDP) alongside your original license. Additionally, you'll need to have **proof of insurance** that covers you for driving in the UK. This could be your own insurance policy that includes **international coverage** or a temporary insurance policy arranged specifically for your stay.

You should also carry **vehicle registration documents** if you're driving a rental car or a vehicle registered in another country. It's a good idea to have a **copy of your passport** and any necessary visas or residency permits, as these may be requested by authorities.

Regarding **toll roads**, the UK has a few toll routes, the most notable being the **M6 Toll Road**. These toll roads typically require payment to use, and the fees can vary depending on the specific route. Payment options generally include cash, credit and debit cards, and some toll booths may accept electronic payments or have a contactless option. For the M6 Toll, you can pay at the booth as you enter or exit, and there are also options for paying online or through mobile apps for convenience. In certain areas, such as London, congestion charges are in place, and payments are usually made online or via designated payment points rather than at toll booths.

 **Main Traffic Rules**

- **Driving side:** Left side of the road

- **Speed limits:**

  - **Urban areas:** 30 mph (48 km/h) unless otherwise specified.
  - **Single carriageway roads:** 60 mph (97 km/h).
  - **Dual carriageways:** 70 mph (113 km/h).
  - **Motorways:** 70 mph (113 km/h).

- **Seat belts:** Mandatory for all passengers. Children under 12 or 135 cm tall must use a child restraint. Failure to wear a seatbelt can result in a £500 (about US$645) fine.

- **Alcohol:** Penalties include fines, points, disqualification, or imprisonment.

  - **England, Wales, Northern Ireland:**0.08% BAC.
  - **Scotland:** 0.05% BAC.

- **Mobile devices:** Using a handheld mobile phone is illegal. Hands-free devices must be used for calls or navigation.

  - **Penalties:** £200 (about US$258) fine and 6 penalty points.

- **Toll roads:** Some roads and tunnels require a toll (e.g., M6 Toll, Dartford Crossing). Payment via cash or electronic systems.

- **If stopped by police:** Pull over safely. Provide driver's license, insurance, MOT, and vehicle ownership documents. Penalties for non-compliance may include fines or arrest.

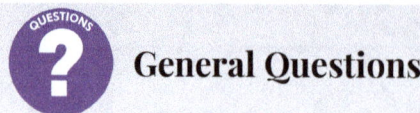

General Questions

1. *Are there any specific rules for using headlights in the UK?*
Yes. In the UK, headlights must be used when driving in poor visibility, such as fog, heavy rain, or snow, and at night. It's also important to use dipped headlights when driving behind another vehicle at night to avoid blinding other drivers. High beam headlights should only be used on dark roads without other vehicles around and should be dipped when approaching oncoming traffic or when following another vehicle.

2. *What is the age requirement for renting a car in the UK?*
The minimum age to rent a car in the UK is typically **21**, though some companies may require renters to be 23 or 25. Drivers under 25 may face higher fees or restrictions on certain vehicles. Most rental companies also require at least 1-2 years of driving experience. International renters may need an international driving permit (IDP) if their licensee is not in English.

3. *Can you drive in bus lanes in the UK?* **No.** In the UK, you are generally **not allowed** to drive in bus lanes unless it's outside the designated operating hours, which are usually indicated by signs. Some bus lanes are in operation 24/7, while others may only be active during peak hours. Driving in a bus lane when it is in operation can result in a fine. Always check the signs to see if and when you are permitted to use the bus lane.

Law of the Land Hypothetical

HYPOTHETICAL: *Tom, a visitor from Germany, is driving in the UK and approaches a pedestrian crossing in a busy city. The traffic light is green, and there are no cars in front of him, so he doesn't stop. However, as he passes the crossing, he notices pedestrians waiting to cross. A traffic warden sees this and stops him. Was Tom breaking the law by not stopping for pedestrians at the crossing, even though the light was green?*

ANSWER: **Yes.** *Tom was breaking the law. In the UK, drivers must always stop for pedestrians waiting to cross at a marked pedestrian crossing, even if the traffic light is green. The green light does not give drivers the right to continue if pedestrians are already on the crossing or waiting to cross. Failing to stop could result in a fine and points on his license and potentially endanger pedestrians. Tom should have yielded to pedestrians as a priority, regardless of the traffic signal.*

NUDE BEACHES & CLOTHING-OPTIONAL RESORTS

NUDE BEACHES & CLOTHING-OPTIONAL RESORTS

Overview

In the UK, nudism, or naturism, is **generally accepted** in certain spaces, though it is **not a widespread cultural practice**. It has a long history in the country, with designated areas and private resorts catering specifically to people who embrace a clothing-free lifestyle. While nudism is not something you would see in everyday public life, it is tolerated and even promoted in specific contexts, such as naturist beaches and private resorts. Public nudity outside these spaces, however, can lead to legal complications, as it may be seen as an offense under the laws governing public decency.

The most **popular nudist beaches** in the UK are typically located in **scenic coastal areas**, where naturism has been practiced for many years. **Brighton Naturist Beach**, located in East Sussex, is one of the best-known nudist beaches, drawing both locals and tourists alike. It's a designated nudist area, meaning that people can visit and enjoy the beach without worrying about the legal implications of being nude in public. Similarly, **Studland Bay** in Dorset is another popular naturist destination, famous for its natural beauty and a long stretch of sand that offers a designated clothing-optional area. Devon is home to **Blackpool Sands**, a beach that, while not officially a nudist spot, is widely recognized as a place where naturists gather, especially in the warmer months. Other locations like **Mersea Island** in Essex and some parts of Scotland, such as the informal beaches near Hedonism in the Scottish Highlands, also provide naturist-friendly spaces.

In addition to beaches, the UK also has a number of **resorts** and **campsites dedicated to nudists**. These venues cater to those seeking a more relaxed, clothing-optional experience. The Naturist Foundation, for instance, is a large organization that manages multiple naturist resorts, including the **Clubhouse** in Kent, where naturists can enjoy various events and activities in a welcoming environment. For those who prefer a more rustic experience, **Sunnydale Farm** in Gloucestershire offers a peaceful, naturist campsite set in the heart of the Cotswolds. Other notable naturist resorts in the UK include **Lupin House** in Hampshire, **Warren Farm** in Somerset, and **The Garden of Eden** in Norfolk. Each of these locations provides a chance for people to enjoy nature and social activities in a relaxed, clothing-optional environment. **Porthkerris**, located in Cornwall, also offers naturist accommodations and a secluded beach for those seeking a quiet retreat.

While these places foster a comfortable and supportive atmosphere for naturists, **public nudity outside of designated areas remains a legal grey area**. The UK has laws around public decency that can result in fines or arrests if an individual is found in violation, particularly if they are causing offense to others. As such, naturism is largely practiced in **private venues**, **organized events**, and **designated areas** like nudist beaches. Public events like the annual **London Naked Bike Ride**, where participants cycle through the city in the nude to raise awareness about environmental and body-positivity issues, help to normalize nudism in certain circles, but they still remain exceptions rather than the norm.

Legality and Safety

Nudism in the UK is regulated by a combination of local government laws, national legislation, and the rules of private spaces. While nudism is **not illegal** per se, there are **strict guidelines** that govern where and how it can be practiced, mainly to prevent issues of public decency and ensure that public spaces remain respectful for everyone. Public nudity is **not generally accepted in non-designated areas**, and the law can be quite clear in defining what constitutes indecent exposure.

In general, the law in the UK states that public nudity **may be considered an offense** if it is done with the intent to cause alarm, distress, or offense to others. This is outlined in the **Indecent Exposure laws**, where people who appear naked in public may be charged under these laws, unless they are in a designated nudist area. In these areas, the practice of nudism is allowed, and the law provides protection for those who choose to be nude.

Designated areas for nudism are typically located on beaches, campsites, and private resorts. Some local councils may establish specific beaches as official "naturist" areas, and these places are where nudism is fully legal. There are also private spaces, such as naturist clubs and resorts, which are governed by their own internal rules and regulations. These private spaces have their own guidelines, which are typically enforced by the facility or the naturist community that operates there.

When it comes to safety, naturists are encouraged to **be respectful of their surroundings** and others while practicing nudism. For example, there are often rules in naturist areas around maintaining a certain level of decorum to ensure that everyone feels comfortable and safe. This includes **being mindful of personal space** and **avoiding lewd or inappropriate behavior.** It is important to remember that nudism is about freedom and relaxation, not about exhibitionism.

In terms of physical safety, naturists are also advised to be cautious about exposure to the sun, as being fully nude increases the risk of sunburn. Sunscreen is strongly recommended, particularly for sensitive areas that are less accustomed to sun exposure. Additionally, some nudist beaches and resorts may have lifeguards or first-aid facilities available, although this varies depending on the location.

Nudist etiquette is based on respect, privacy, and appropriate behavior. It's important to avoid staring at others and to respect their personal space. Photography is usually prohibited in naturist areas to ensure everyone feels comfortable. Nudism is meant to be **non-sexual**, and any inappropriate behavior can lead to being asked to leave. **Maintaining hygiene** is also crucial; it's common to sit on towels or mats and to shower before using communal pools. While nudity is allowed in designated areas, clothing may be required in places like restaurants or shops, so it's essential to follow the dress codes of each location. The naturist community values friendliness and inclusiveness, so newcomers should feel welcomed and respected. Lastly, it's important to **respect the environment** by keeping natural spaces clean and avoiding littering. These simple rules help ensure a respectful and enjoyable experience for everyone.

 **General Questions**

1. *Are there any age restrictions or family-friendly policies at nudist beaches and clothing-optional resorts in the UK?*
   No. Nudist beaches and clothing-optional resorts in the UK are family-friendly and welcome visitors of all ages. These locations often have specific areas designated for families, where children can enjoy the natural environment in a safe and respectful atmosphere. Family policies usually emphasize that nudism is non-sexual, ensuring that children can experience naturism in a comfortable setting. Some resorts even offer child-friendly activities, such as swimming lessons or nature walks. However, age restrictions may apply to certain private resorts or events, with some venues being adults-only to maintain a more serene or exclusive atmosphere. It's always recommended to check individual resort policies before visiting.

2. ***How do clothing-optional resorts in the UK handle privacy and security for guests?*** Clothing-optional resorts in the UK prioritize privacy and security by implementing strict rules and measures to ensure a safe and respectful environment for all guests. Many resorts operate on a members-only or pre-booked basis, which helps control access and ensures that everyone is there for the same purpose. These resorts often have gated entrances, on-site security, and surveillance to maintain safety. Additionally, privacy is respected with clear guidelines on behavior, including restrictions on photography and rules that prevent unwanted attention.

Law of the Land Hypothetical

HYPOTHETICAL: *John, a first-time naturist, has recently joined a naturist resort in Devon for a weekend getaway. The resort has a strict "clothing-optional" policy, allowing guests to choose when and where to be nude. After a day of sunbathing, John decides to go for a swim in the resort's pool, which is designated as a clothing-optional area. However, upon arrival, he notices a group of people who are not only fully clothed but seem to be violating the resort's rules by engaging in inappropriate sexual behavior. John feels uncomfortable and wonders if he has any legal grounds to report this situation.*

ANSWER: ***Yes.*** *John can report inappropriate behavior. Clothing-optional resorts in the UK have strict rules prohibiting sexual activity in public spaces. John should report the situation to resort management, who can enforce the rules and ask the offenders to leave. If the behavior is severe, John can contact local authorities, as public sexual activity can lead to legal consequences under indecency or public order laws. The resort is responsible for maintaining a respectful, non-sexual environment for all guests.*

CHAPTER 20
UNUSUAL LAWS

UNUSUAL LAWS

Overview

Unusual laws can be fascinating glimpses into a culture's values and history. While most people are aware of common legal restrictions, it's often the strange and quirky laws that capture our attention. These regulations can range from the amusing to the absurd, reflecting the unique circumstances and traditions of a place. Whether they arise from historical events, societal norms, or simply peculiar local customs, unusual laws can provide insight into the quirks of human behavior and governance.

 **Unusual Laws in the UK and Associated Penalties**

The UK has a number of quirky and unusual laws that often seem outdated or odd, yet technically still exist in the legal system. While many of these laws are rarely enforced, they continue to spark curiosity. Here are a few examples:

It's Illegal to Die in the Houses of Parliament

One of the most famous and peculiar laws in the UK is that it is illegal to die in the Houses of Parliament. While this law has little to no practical enforcement, it's often cited as a fun quirk of British law.

The law is effectively unenforceable. If someone were to die in the Houses of Parliament, their death would likely be treated the same as any other death and investigated by the authorities, but there's no specific penalty attached to this "crime."

It's Illegal to Handle a Salmon Under Suspicious Circumstances

Under the **Salmon Act of 1986**, it is illegal to handle a salmon in suspicious circumstances. This bizarre law was put in place to combat illegal fishing practices and the trade of salmon.

Violators can be fined **up to £5,000** (about US$6,464) or face **up to two years** in prison for handling salmon in a way that raises suspicion of illegal activity. This could involve possessing a salmon that's believed to have been caught illegally or without proper documentation.

It's Illegal to Enter the Houses of Parliament in a Suit of Armor

The **Parliament Acts** state that no one is allowed to enter the Houses of Parliament in a suit of armor. This law dates back to medieval times when knights would be barred from entering for safety reasons, but it's still technically on the books today.

There is no clear penalty for this, but any attempt to enter the Houses of Parliament while dressed in armor would almost certainly result in a refusal of entry or arrest on the grounds of disruptive behavior or security concerns.

It's Illegal to Be Drunk While in Charge of a Cow

Under the **Licensing Act of 1872**, it is an offense to be drunk while in charge of a cow. This law was likely intended to prevent accidents in rural areas, especially when cows were more commonly used for milk production and transportation.

Violators could face a **fine** or **imprisonment**, although enforcement is virtually non-existent today. Being found drunk in charge of a cow may also result in charges for public intoxication.

It's Illegal to Peep into Someone's Window with a Telescope

Under **common law**, it is illegal to peep into someone's window with a telescope. This is part of privacy protection, designed to prevent invasion of people's private lives through the use of surveillance tools.

If caught in the act, offenders could be charged with harassment, breach of privacy, or voyeurism, depending on the circumstances. Penalties include **fines**, **imprisonment**, or a **restraining order**.

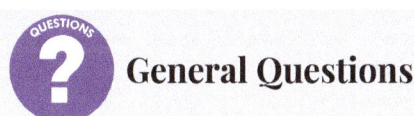 **General Questions**

1. *Is it illegal to be drunk in charge of a car in the UK, even if you're not driving?* **Yes.** Under the **Road Traffic Act of 1988**, it is illegal to be in charge of a vehicle while drunk, even if you're not driving. Being in charge means having control over the vehicle, such as sitting in the driver's seat with the keys in your possession. If the police believe you could drive the vehicle while intoxicated, you can face penalties such as fines, a driving ban, or imprisonment, even if you weren't actually driving.

2. *Is it illegal to be naked in your own home in the UK?* **No.** It is not illegal to be naked in your own home in the UK. However, if your nakedness is visible from outside and causes alarm or distress to others, you could be charged with public indecency or harassment. So, while you are free to be naked inside your own home, it's important to ensure that your actions don't unintentionally breach the peace or violate others' sense of privacy.

3. *Is it illegal to walk your sheep down the street in the UK?* **Yes.** Under an old law in London's city statutes, it is technically illegal to drive sheep down certain streets without permission. This law dates back to when livestock could cause damage to the roads and traffic. Although not enforced today, it still exists in some legal texts as a quirky remnant of historical regulations.

CHAPTER 21

TRAVELING SAFELY

TRAVELING SAFELY

Ladies Traveling Solo

The United Kingdom is generally regarded as a **safe destination** for travelers, including women traveling alone. It has a strong reputation for public safety, well-developed infrastructure, and a relatively **low overall crime rate** compared to many other countries. However, like any place, safety can vary depending on the area and the time of day.

For women traveling alone, the UK is often seen as a safe and welcoming place. Many solo female travelers visit the country without issues. British cities are usually very well-policed, with excellent transport networks and a culture that is generally supportive of solo travel. While it's relatively safe to explore most areas, there are still some **precautions** to take. For example, it's advisable not to walk alone late at night in poorly lit or unfamiliar areas. Also, it's important to keep personal belongings secure in busy areas, such as train stations or popular tourist spots. If something feels off, it's always best to trust your instincts and move to a more populated or well-lit area. Using official taxis or rideshare services like Uber is a good idea, particularly after dark.

Major cities like London, Manchester, and Edinburgh are popular with tourists and have areas that are generally safe for solo female travelers. London, as the capital, is a bustling metropolis, and its main tourist districts like Westminster, Covent Garden, and Soho are very safe and well-policed. However, there are neighborhoods such as parts of **Hackney** or **Tottenham** that are known for higher crime rates. Although these areas can be fine during the day, caution is advised when visiting them **after dark**. Similarly, Manchester has vibrant areas like Deansgate and the Northern Quarter, but neighborhoods like **Gorton** and **Cheetham Hill** may require more awareness, especially at night. In Edinburgh, the city center is very safe, and it's a popular destination for solo travelers, but it's always wise to exercise general caution in less well-populated areas after dark.

 ## Safety Precautions

Here are some safety precautions to take as a female solo traveler in the UK:

- **Stay aware of your surroundings:** When traveling alone, especially in busy areas like train stations, markets, or tourist attractions, it's important to be aware of what's happening around you. Avoid getting distracted by your phone or other devices when walking in public spaces.

- **Keep your belongings secure:** Pickpocketing can occur in crowded areas, so keep your bags and valuables close to your body. Consider using a crossbody bag with a zip or a money belt. Avoid carrying large amounts of cash or flashy jewelry that could attract unwanted attention.

- **Avoid poorly lit or deserted areas at night:** While many parts of UK cities are safe, some areas can feel less secure, especially after dark. Avoid walking alone in poorly lit streets or areas that seem deserted. Stick to well-populated places, and if you need to get somewhere after dark, consider using a taxi, rideshare service (like Uber), or public transport instead.

- **Use reliable transport services:** Public transportation in the UK is generally safe, but it's still a good idea to avoid empty trains or buses, especially late at night. If you're using taxis, make sure they are licensed, or consider booking through a reputable rideshare app like Uber.

- **Trust your instincts:** If something doesn't feel right, leave the area and find somewhere safe. Trusting your gut is one of the most important tools for staying safe. If you feel uncomfortable, look for a nearby shop, cafe, or public space where you can seek assistance.

- **Stay connected:** Share your travel plans and itinerary with a family member or friend before your trip. Let someone know where you are going and when you expect to return, especially if you're heading to a less populated area or out late at night.

- **Know emergency numbers:** In the UK, the emergency services number is **999**, whether you're dealing with police, medical, or fire emergencies. It's good to know this number in case you need it.

- **Plan ahead:** Research the places you're visiting in advance to know which areas are safer, especially at night. Some districts, particularly in larger cities, may have higher crime rates or be less safe after dark.

- **Stay in reputable accommodations:** Whether you're staying in a hotel, guesthouse, or Airbnb, make sure your accommodation is well-reviewed and in a safe neighborhood. Choose locations close to public transportation or main tourist areas for added convenience and safety.

By following these simple safety precautions, solo female travelers can have a positive and secure experience in the UK. Always remember to trust your instincts, stay alert, and enjoy your travels with peace of mind.

Traveling as a Family

Traveling with children in the UK can be a rewarding experience, with many family-friendly attractions and well-developed infrastructure.

However, when traveling with young ones, it's important to take certain safety and health precautions.

In busy places like train stations and popular tourist spots, always keep a close eye on your children. Consider using child harnesses or wrist straps for younger kids and teach older children to stay close. It's also important to educate them about **road safety**, as UK cities can be busy with heavy traffic. Make sure they understand how to cross streets safely and stay close to an adult.

Public transportation is a great way to get around the UK but always plan ahead. On the London Underground and buses, use priority seating areas designed for families. For trains, reserving a family compartment offers more space. If you're renting a car, ensure you have an appropriate **car seat**, as UK law requires children under 12 or shorter than 135 cm (53 inches) to use one.

When choosing accommodations, opt for **child-friendly hotels or rentals** that offer amenities like baby cots or safety features such as child-proof windows. Always check reviews and ensure the area is secure. It's also a good idea to have a list of emergency contacts and ensure your child knows what to do if they get lost.

If your child becomes ill, the UK offers excellent healthcare, and **children under 16 can receive free medical care** from the NHS. Make sure to have travel insurance that covers health and emergencies. Carry a basic medical kit with any necessary medications and be mindful of food allergies or dietary restrictions. While food and water safety are generally good in the UK, it's always a good idea to ask about ingredients in restaurants, especially for children with allergies.

Supervise children around water, whether at the beach or by lakes, and always ensure they have proper flotation devices. Make sure to apply sunscreen regularly, even on cloudy days, and encourage hydration throughout the day, particularly in warmer weather.

Finally, plan your itinerary with plenty of breaks to keep children rested and entertained. The UK offers numerous child-friendly museums, parks, and attractions, making it easy for families to explore and enjoy together. With the right preparation, the UK can be a fantastic and safe destination for family travel.

Advice for All Travelers

Traveling in the UK is generally safe, but there are a few things to be cautious about. **Pickpocketing** and **theft** can occur, especially in crowded tourist spots, public transport, and shopping districts. Keep your belongings secure and stay vigilant in busy areas like train stations or on the London Underground.

Be mindful of **road safety** as the UK drives on the left-hand side. Pay attention when crossing streets, as traffic may not always stop immediately. Certain areas, especially after dark, can feel less safe, so it's a good idea to use public transport or rideshare services at night.

The **weather** in the UK is **unpredictable**, so always carry an umbrella or waterproof jacket. During winter, be cautious of icy conditions on roads and paths, especially in rural areas. While **food safety** is high, be cautious with street food vendors. Research where to eat and be mindful of food allergies. Watch out for tourist traps in popular areas, where prices can be inflated, and consider exploring less crowded locations for better deals.

Finally, **public toilets** may be scarce in some areas, especially in smaller towns. Be prepared to pay a small fee or plan ahead when exploring remote locations. Staying aware of these factors will help ensure a safe and enjoyable trip.

Do's and Don'ts While in the UK

- **Do:** Embrace the British culture of queuing. Always stand in line and wait your turn, whether at the bus stop, in a shop, or at an attraction. It's an important part of British politeness.

- **Don't:** Assume you can walk straight across the road without checking traffic first, even in pedestrian areas. Cars in the UK drive on the left, so always be cautious when crossing streets.

- **Do:** Embrace the pub culture. Pubs are a great place to socialize and experience British life. It's customary to order your drinks at the bar rather than waiting for table service.

- **Don't:** Engage in excessive public displays of affection. While holding hands or a quick kiss is fine, more intimate displays are generally frowned upon in public places.

- **Do:** Be punctual. The British value timeliness, especially for meetings or social events. If you're running late, it's polite to let the other person know.

- **Don't:** Rush your meals. Dining in the UK is often a leisurely, social experience. Take your time and enjoy the food and conversation.

- **Do:** Respect historical sites. The UK is full of ancient landmarks and monuments, so be mindful not to climb on or damage anything.

- **Don't:** Take photos in places where it's not allowed. Many museums and galleries have restrictions on photography, so always check signs or ask permission before snapping a picture.

- **Do:** Tip appropriately. Tipping is expected for services, typically around 10-15 percent in restaurants, and rounding up for taxi rides is also appreciated.

- **Don't:** Over-tip. While tipping is appreciated, it's not customary to leave large tips. A 10-15 percent tip is standard in most situations.

- **Do:** Carry both cash and cards. While cards are widely accepted, it's good to have some cash on hand for smaller purchases or tips.

- **Don't:** Expect free tap water in all restaurants. While some places will offer it, you may be charged for bottled water in others, particularly in pubs.

- **Do:** Plan for unpredictable weather. The UK is known for its sudden changes in weather, so always carry an umbrella or waterproof jacket, especially in the spring and autumn.

- **Don't:** Underestimate how expensive things can be. London, in particular, can be costly, so plan ahead and check prices, especially for attractions and dining.

To engage with the local culture in the UK respectfully, focus on being polite and considerate. Use "please," "thank you," and "sorry," and be mindful of personal space, as the British value their privacy. When conversing, stick to light topics like the weather and avoid sensitive subjects like politics unless you know the person well. Embrace the British love of queuing and always wait your turn. Show interest in local traditions but avoid being overly personal. Understand that British humor can be dry and sarcastic, so don't take it literally. Lastly, be punctual, as being late is often seen as disrespectful.

CHAPTER 22

TOURIST TAXATION

TOURIST TAXATION

Overview

Tourism plays **a significant role** in the UK economy, providing both financial gains and job opportunities. In 2023, tourism accounted for about **£239 billion** (about US$309.4 billion) of the UK's GDP, representing nearly 9.7 percent of the nation's total economic output.[34] This industry directly employs around 1.7 million people, which is about 5.3 percent of the workforce.[35] The UK is a major global tourism destination, attracting millions of international visitors each year, while domestic tourism also represents a large market. Major tourist cities like London, along with scenic regions such as Cornwall and the Lake District, benefit greatly from the economic activity generated by tourism.

In response to the challenges brought about by increasing tourist numbers, some local authorities in the UK have introduced tourist taxation. This tax involves levying a fee on visitors when they book short-term accommodations such as hotels, hostels, or bed-and-breakfasts. The revenue generated from these taxes is used to support local infrastructure, manage tourism effectively, and enhance public services that often struggle with higher visitor volumes. For instance, cities like Manchester and Liverpool have implemented visitor levies that help fund local tourism

---

34 https://www.statista.com/statistics/598093/
    travel-and-tourism-gdp-total-contribution-united-kingdom-uk/

35 https://commonslibrary.parliament.uk/research-briefings/sn06022/

initiatives while ensuring that local residents are not solely responsible for the costs associated with increased tourism.[36]

Overall, tourist taxation serves **multiple objectives**. It generates essential funds for local governments and assists in managing the impact of high visitor numbers. Additionally, it aims to improve the experiences of those visiting these areas by channeling the collected funds back into local communities. However, discussions surrounding tourist taxation continue, as some argue that while it promotes sustainable tourism, others worry that it may discourage visitors, especially in an already challenging economic environment. Thus, the integration of tourist taxes into the UK's tourism strategy is viewed as a crucial step in balancing the positive and negative aspects of a growing tourism economy.

Tourist Taxes in the UK

In the UK, there is no national tourist tax, but several taxes and fees apply to tourists, helping to manage the impact of tourism on local infrastructure and services.

One of the most common taxes tourists pay is **Value Added Tax (VAT)**, which is included in the price of most goods and services, such as accommodation, meals, and transportation. The standard VAT rate is **20 percent**, but certain goods like food, children's clothing, and books are subject to a reduced rate of 5 percent. (https://wise.com/gb/vat/)

Another key tax affecting tourists is **Air Passenger Duty (APD)**, a tax levied on all passengers flying out of the UK. The amount depends on the destination and class of travel, with higher rates for long-haul flights and premium cabins. APD is included in the price of airline tickets, so passengers effectively pay it when purchasing their flights. The airline collects the tax and passes it on to the government.[37]

---

36 https://www.theguardian.com/travel/2024/nov/24/
     millions-of-tourists-in-uk-could-be-asked-to-pay-local-visitor-levy

37 https://www.fccaviation.com/resources/uk-apd-the-ultimate-guide

In some areas, especially those with high tourist traffic, local authorities may impose **accommodation taxes**. These small surcharges are typically added to the cost of hotel stays and other types of accommodation. While the UK does not have a nationwide tourist tax, cities like Edinburgh have discussed or introduced **local taxes** to help fund infrastructure projects and services affected by tourism. These accommodation taxes are usually charged per night of stay, and the hotel or property owner collects and remits the fee to the local government.

Congestion charges are another form of tax that affects tourists, particularly in cities like London. The congestion charge applies to vehicles driving into certain high-traffic areas, such as central London. Tourists driving into these zones are required to pay a daily fee, usually **around £15** (about US$19). The fee helps manage traffic congestion and is paid either online, via mobile apps, or at designated payment points.

Though the UK does not have a single national tourist tax, a combination of VAT, air passenger duties, local accommodation taxes, and other fees help fund public services, infrastructure, and manage the impact of tourism on local communities. These taxes and fees are designed to ensure that visitors contribute to the maintenance and development of the places they visit.

 ## Law of the Land Hypothetical

HYPOTHETICAL: *Lena, a Canadian tourist, books a flight from Toronto to Tokyo with a layover in London. Her ticket includes Air Passenger Duty (APD), but Lena does not leave the airport during the layover. Is Lena required to pay APD on her connecting flight if she doesn't leave the airport in London?*

ANSWER: *Lena should **not** pay APD. APD is only charged on flights departing the UK to international destinations, not for passengers merely transiting through the UK without leaving the airport. Since Lena is not departing the UK, the APD charge should not apply. She* *can contact the airline to request a refund for the APD portion of her ticket. If the airline refuses, she may file a complaint with the UK Civil Aviation Authority (CAA).*

LONG-TERM STAYS

LONG-TERM STAYS

Overview

Long-term migration to the UK has been a hot topic, especially after recent changes in immigration rules. According to the Office for National Statistics (ONS), around 1.2 million people moved to the UK in the year ending June 2024 , resulting in a net migration figure of 728,000, which is quite high.[38] This situation reflects a growing trend of foreign residents in the UK, particularly after Brexit. Most new long-term migrants are from non-EU countries, making up 86 percent of the total. Only 10 percent are EU nationals, and about 5 percent are British nationals returning to live permanently. This shift became noticeable after the UK introduced a new immigration system in January 2021, which made it harder for EU citizens to move to the UK compared to before. Indian nationals have become the largest group among those immigrating to the UK, accounting for 20 percent of new arrivals.[39]

People choose to stay long-term in the UK for various reasons, including work opportunities, educational prospects, cultural experiences, and

---

38 https://www.ons.gov.uk/peoplepopulationandcommunity/
    populationandmigration/internationalmigration/bulletins/
    longterminternationalmigrationprovisional/yearendingdecember2023

39 https://www.ons.gov.uk/peoplepopulationandcommunity/
    populationandmigration/internationalmigration/bulletins/
    longterminternationalmigrationprovisional/yearendingjune2024

a high quality of life. One of the main draws is the UK's **vibrant job market**, particularly in sectors like finance, technology, healthcare, and education. Cities such as London, Manchester, and Edinburgh offer diverse career prospects, attracting professionals and entrepreneurs from around the world. Additionally, the UK's **rich cultural and historical heritage** is a significant factor for many expatriates. The country's access to world-class museums, theaters, historical landmarks, and its multicultural environment make it a compelling place to live for those interested in both modern urban living and traditional European culture. The allure of the UK's lifestyle, with its unique blend of cosmopolitan city life and access to nature, is a major motivator for long-term residents.

The country's **education system** also attracts people looking to pursue higher education. With prestigious universities like **Oxford**, **Cambridge**, and **Imperial College London**, the UK is a hub for academic excellence. Many international students decide to stay in the country after graduation due to the excellent job prospects and the chance to continue their professional growth in a globally recognized market. Furthermore, the **quality and accessibility of healthcare** in the UK, especially through the National Health Service (NHS), is a critical reason why many people choose to remain in the country long-term.

When it comes to the **best places** for long-term stays in the UK, it largely depends on individual preferences, lifestyle, and career goals. **London**, being the capital, is a natural choice for those seeking a bustling, cosmopolitan environment with an abundance of job opportunities, cultural events, shopping, and entertainment. It's ideal for people who thrive in a fast-paced, international setting. For those who prefer a more relaxed pace but still want access to many of the country's advantages, cities like **Manchester** and **Bristol** provide a balance between affordability and urban living. These cities have burgeoning tech sectors, creative industries, and vibrant cultural scenes. **Edinburgh**, with its historical significance and stunning architecture, appeals to those looking for a quieter, more scenic lifestyle, while still offering excellent job prospects, especially in the fields of education, technology, and finance.

For those seeking **more affordable options**, regions outside the major urban centers, such as the North East of England or Wales, provide lower living costs and a slower pace of life, with easy access to nature and historical landmarks. Cities like **Newcastle** or **Cardiff** are gaining popularity due to their lower housing costs, strong job markets, and access to a rich cultural life. Ultimately, the best location for a long-term stay in the UK depends on what an individual values most, whether it's career growth, cultural engagement, or a quieter lifestyle.

Living Costs in the UK

Living costs in the UK can **vary significantly** depending on the region and lifestyle, but overall, it tends to be expensive, particularly in major cities like London. For those considering long-term stays, it's important to be aware of the general cost breakdown for housing, food, utilities, and transportation:

- **Housing Costs:** Rent in London can range from £1,500 to £2,500 per month (approximately US$1,800 to $3,000), with central areas being more expensive. Outside London, rents are more affordable, with cities like Manchester and Birmingham offering apartments for £600 to £1,200 (about US$720 to $1,440). In rural areas, rents can start from £400 to £700 (roughly US$480 to $840). Initial costs like deposits and agency fees should also be considered.

- **Utilities:** Monthly utilities typically cost between £100 and £200 (around US$120 to $240), depending on the property size and location. Internet and mobile plans are generally affordable, with internet costing £25–£40 (about US$30 to $48) and mobile plans starting at £10–£30 (approximately US$12 to $36) per month.

- **Food Costs:** Grocery shopping ranges from £150 to £300 per month (around US$180 to $360). Dining out at mid-range restaurants typically costs £15–£30 per person (roughly US$18 to $36), while casual dining or takeaways range from £5 to £10 (about US$6 to $12). Imported goods and high-end restaurants can increase food costs.

- **Transportation Costs:** In London, a monthly travel card can cost £150–£250 (approximately US$180 to $300), depending on the zones. In other cities like Manchester and Birmingham, monthly passes range from £50 to £100 (roughly US$60 to $120).

Healthcare For Long-Term Residents

The UK's healthcare system, primarily through the National Health Service (NHS), is a major attraction for long-term residents. The NHS provides **free** or **subsidized** primary care, hospital, and emergency services, funded through taxes and National Insurance contributions from workers. While most services are free at the point of use, treatments like dental care, optical services, and prescriptions may require payment, though they are subsidized. Private healthcare options are available but can be expensive. Long-term residents, including those on work visas or permanent residency, are eligible for NHS services, though newcomers may need to pay the Immigration Health Surcharge as part of their visa process.[40]

Housing Options for Long-Term Stays

Housing options in the UK vary significantly depending on location, and the choice largely depends on an individual's lifestyle and budget. In urban centers like London, Manchester, and Edinburgh, the most common housing options are private apartments and shared accommodations. **Renting an apartment** in a city center is the most typical choice for expatriates, although **shared flats** or houses are common for those looking to reduce costs. In rural areas or smaller towns, long-term residents might choose **detached houses** or smaller flats, and housing is generally more affordable than in major cities.

There are also options like house shares or even **renting a room** in a shared house, which is particularly popular among students and young professionals. Those looking for a more unique or traditional living experience can opt for **renting a cottage** or a home in the countryside, where housing costs are significantly lower than in urban centers.

---

40 https://www.gov.uk/healthcare-immigration-application/how-much-pay

Transportation Options

The UK offers an extensive and reliable transportation network. In major cities, public transport is the most common and efficient way to get around. The **London Underground** (**Tube**) is one of the most famous metro systems in the world, and cities like Manchester and Glasgow also have well-established **bus**, **tram**, and **metro networks**. In addition to these, **train** travel is commonly used for intercity travel, particularly in the form of high-speed services like the East Coast Main Line and the West Coast Main Line.

For residents outside of major cities, owning a **car** is often necessary, as public transport options may be limited. However, driving in larger cities like London can be expensive due to congestion charges and limited parking. Many long-term residents opt for public transportation, cycling, or walking as their primary modes of getting around.

Language Considerations

The primary language spoken in the UK is **English**, which makes it an attractive destination for those fluent in the language. However, the UK is home to **many regional dialects** and **accents**, which may take some getting used to. In urban areas like London, it's common to hear **multiple languages** spoken, as the city is home to diverse international communities. While English is widely understood throughout the country, learning regional dialects and expressions can help long-term residents integrate more easily into their local communities. Understanding British English, including slang and idioms, can be crucial for both social interactions and professional settings.

For non-native English speakers, learning the language is highly recommended for those looking to live in the UK long-term, as it will help with everything from professional advancement to day-to-day activities such as shopping, banking, and navigating public transport. Many local communities offer free or subsidized English language classes to help newcomers improve their skills and ease their transition into life in the UK.

Long-Term Visas[41]

The UK offers several visa options for individuals seeking long-term stays, catering to different purposes such as work, study, family reunification, and investment. Here are the main categories:

- **Work Visas:** The **Skilled Worker Visa** is the most common for professionals who have a job offer from a UK employer in a skilled occupation. It allows individuals to stay for up to five years, with the possibility of extending or applying for settlement (indefinite leave to remain). Other work-related visas include the **Global Talent Visa**, designed for highly skilled individuals in fields like technology, science, and the arts, and the **Health and Care Worker Visa**, specifically for medical professionals.

- **Student Visas:** The **Student Visa** allows international students to study in the UK for the duration of their course, typically up to five years. Post-study options like the **Graduate Visa** (for up to two years) enable graduates to remain in the UK to work or look for work in any field.

- **Family Visas:** Individuals wishing to join family members in the UK can apply for a **Family Visa**, which includes spouse, partner, or dependent child visas. These visas typically grant permission to stay for two-and-a-half to five years, with the possibility of extension and eventual settlement.

- **Investor, Business, and Entrepreneur Visas:** The **Innovator Visa** and **Start-up Visa** are available for individuals wishing to establish or run a business in the UK. The **Investor Visa** allows those with substantial financial resources—usually £2 million (about US$2.59 million), or more—to invest in the UK economy for a minimum of two years, with the possibility of settlement.

- **Settlement and Indefinite Leave to Remain (ILR):** After living in the UK for a qualifying period (usually five years, depending on the visa type), individuals may apply for **Indefinite Leave to Remain (ILR)**, which grants permanent residency. This is often a step toward eventual British citizenship.

---

41 https://getgoldenvisa.com/uk-visa-types-and-immigration

 For more information on visas, requirements, and fees, please visit the UK's official Visas and Immigration website at **https://www.gov.uk/government/organisations/uk-visas-and-immigration**.

 **General Questions**

1. *If I want to stay in the UK for long-term and work, should I apply for a work permit before arriving in the UK?* **Yes**. If you want to work in the UK long-term, you must apply for a work visa before arriving. The most common option is the Skilled Worker Visa, which requires a confirmed job offer from a UK employer who can sponsor you. You'll need to meet certain eligibility criteria, such as having a job that meets skill and salary requirements and proving English proficiency. The visa must be approved before you travel, as you cannot legally work in the UK without it. The application process can take several weeks, so it's best to apply well in advance.

2. *I am American. Can I retire to the UK?* **Yes**. As an American, you can retire to the UK, but there isn't a specific retirement visa. You can consider a Standard Visitor Visa, which allows stays of up to six months but doesn't permit long-term residency or work. If you have family in the UK, you may qualify for a Family Visa, which can lead to long-term residency. Another option is the Tier 1 Investor Visa, available if you have significant financial resources—usually £2 million (about US$2.59) or more—allowing you to live and invest in the UK. While there's no direct retirement visa, these routes may allow you to retire in the UK, depending on your circumstances.

Law of the Land Hypothetical

HYPOTHETICAL: *Sarah, a U.S. citizen, has been living and working in the UK on a Skilled Worker Visa for the past four years. She is employed as a software engineer at a tech company in London and recently got married to a British citizen. Can Sarah apply for permanent residency in the UK after her Skilled Worker Visa expires, and how will her marriage to a British citizen affect the process?*

ANSWER: ***Yes****. Sarah can apply for **Indefinite Leave to Remain (ILR)** after holding a Skilled Worker Visa for five years, provided she meets the necessary requirements, including proving her employment, salary, and meeting the English language and residency criteria. Since she's already been in the UK for four years, she will need one more year on her current visa before applying.*

*While being married to a British citizen could allow her to apply for ILR under the **Spouse Visa** route, it's generally faster to continue with the Skilled Worker Visa path for ILR. Therefore, unless there's a specific reason to switch to a Spouse Visa, Sarah should remain on her current visa to apply for ILR after five years.*

Law of the Land True Story[42]

Sally, a U.S. citizen living in the UK, faced a series of challenges that led to her becoming an overstayer. After her job offer was withdrawn during the pandemic, and with her visa set to expire amid the lockdown, she struggled to find a way to regularize her status. The pandemic had already drained her savings, and without the right legal guidance, Sally unknowingly missed the opportunity to apply for a family visa based on her unmarried partnership with Kevin, her British partner. As a

---

42 https://www.edgewaterlegal.com/insight/
    case-notes-application-by-overstayer-to-regularise-stay/

result, she became an overstayer, a situation that would trigger a long and difficult legal battle.

This case illustrates the devastating impact of overstaying a visa in the UK. Overstayers often find themselves facing prolonged legal processes, loss of income, and a range of personal hardships. In Sally's case, the Home Office initially insisted that she apply from her home country, despite the exceptional circumstances of her mental health and Kevin's disability. After months of legal challenges, including an appeal, Sally was granted permission to stay for another two-and-a-half years, but the process took almost two years in total.

Sally's experience underscores the serious risks of overstaying a visa in the UK. Legal pathways to regularization are often complex and time-consuming, with no guarantee of success. This story serves as a stark reminder of the challenges that come with overstaying, and the critical importance of adhering to visa deadlines to avoid lengthy delays, emotional strain, and potential financial ruin.

CHAPTER 24

CIVIL LITIGATION

IN THIS CHAPTER

- Overview
- Personal Injury Claims and Compensation Law
- How to File a Civil Claim
- Service of Documents
- Statute of Limitations
- Getting Married in the UK
- Law of the Land Hypothetical

CIVIL LITIGATION

Overview

Civil litigation provides a mechanism for resolving disputes, ensuring that travelers have a way to seek justice if legal issues arise while visiting another country. It helps them understand their rights and obligations under local laws, which may differ from those in their home country. The civil litigation system offers a formal process for addressing conflicts, such as contract disputes or personal injury claims, and can deter unfair practices by encouraging businesses to comply with legal standards. It also allows individuals to seek financial recourse for damages or losses and helps protect them from potential exploitation by local entities. Overall, understanding civil litigation enhances a visitor's experience and safety while traveling.

Personal Injury Claims and Compensation Law [43]

In the UK, personal injury claims serve as a vital avenue for individuals seeking compensation when they suffer harm due to someone else's negligence. A personal injury claim often arises from various grounds, including **accidents at work**, **road traffic accidents**, **medical negligence**, or **injuries sustained in public places**. When pursuing a personal injury

---

43 https://www.citizensadvice.org.uk/law-and-courts/
claiming-compensation-for-a-personal-injury/personal-injuries/)

claim, the essential factor is proving that the injury was caused by a breach of duty of care on the part of another person or organization. This means that if someone fails to act reasonably and their actions result in injury, those affected may have the right to seek compensation for their suffering.

If you've been injured due to an accident or someone else's negligence, you might be wondering about your options for compensation. Essentially, if someone else is at fault, you have the right to seek compensation for the pain, suffering, and financial loss caused by the injury. The first thing you should do after an injury is **seek medical attention**. Your health and safety should always come first. Once you've seen a doctor or visited the hospital, it's important to **gather evidence**, like photographs of the injury, witness statements, and any other details about how the accident happened. This will be vital for your claim. You should also **report the incident** to the relevant authorities, whether it's the police for an accident or a workplace injury report for a work-related incident. Having a clear record of what happened will help strengthen your case.

When it comes to calculating damages, the amount you could receive will depend on the severity of your injury, how it's affected your life, and any costs you've incurred. Generally, damages are divided into two types: **general damages**, which compensate for the pain, suffering, and loss of quality of life, and **special damages**, which cover financial losses like medical bills, lost wages, or the cost of rehabilitation. Your lawyer can help you estimate what you're entitled to based on these factors.

Insurance often plays a big role in personal injury claims. If the person responsible for the injury has insurance (for example, car insurance or public liability insurance), you may make a claim against their insurance policy. In some cases, you might also have your own insurance that can help cover medical costs or lost income during your recovery. If you're in an accident and the responsible party is uninsured or underinsured, you might need to claim from your own policy or through a government fund, depending on the situation.

As for the **legal fees** involved, it's common to worry about how much it will cost to pursue a claim. In the UK, many personal injury lawyers work on a **no-win, no-fee** basis. This means that if you don't win your case, you won't have to pay any legal fees. However, if you win, the lawyer will typically take a percentage of the compensation as their fee. There may also be other costs, such as court fees or expenses for expert witnesses, but these are usually covered under no-win, no-fee agreements or can be recovered as part of your compensation.

As a visitor in the UK, you are entitled to compensation for personal injury if you are injured due to someone else's fault or negligence. Whether you're a tourist, student, or any other type of visitor, UK law allows you to make a claim for injuries caused by accidents. **Visitors have the same legal rights as UK residents in pursuing compensation.** However, practical considerations like whether you have travel insurance, and where you're from, may affect how the claim is handled. There is also a **time limit** for making a claim, typically **three years from the date of the accident** or from when you first realized the injury was linked to the incident.

How to File a Civil Claim

Filing a civil claim in the UK involves a structured process designed to resolve disputes between individuals, organizations, or between an individual and an organization. To file a claim, there are certain requirements and steps you must follow.

To begin with, you need to have a **valid legal basis for the claim**. This means you must demonstrate that you have been wronged or harmed in a way that the law recognizes as grounds for compensation or remedy. This could involve issues like **breach of contract, personal injury, property damage**, or **employment disputes**, among others. It's important to gather all the facts, evidence, and documentation that support your claim.

The **location** where your claim should be filed depends on the value and type of your case. For smaller claims, typically valued **under £10,000** (about US$12,935), you can file with the **Small Claims Court**, which is part of the County Court system. For larger, more complex cases, the **High Court** or **County Court** may be the appropriate venue. If the case involves specific areas like **family law**, there are designated **Family Courts**. In certain cases, such as claims related to housing or employment, **special tribunals** may be required.

The process starts by determining the **type of claim** you're making. Whether it's a personal injury case, a breach of contract, or a debt recovery issue, identifying the nature of your claim is crucial because it will dictate the forms you need and where you file your claim. Once you know the type of claim, the next step is to figure out which court is appropriate. For smaller claims, typically **up to £10,000** (about US$12,935), you can use the **Money Claim Online** (**MCOL**) service. This is a straightforward, online process. If your claim is **between £10,000 and £25,000** (about US$12,935 and $32,332), you'll need to use the **Money Claims Service**, which also allows you to submit your claim online. For larger claims, **over £25,000** (about US$32,332), you will need to use **Form N1**, a paper claim form that you download from the GOV.UK website.[44]

After selecting the correct court and form, the next task is to complete the claim form with accurate details. For online claims, you simply fill out the form on the relevant website. If you're using **Form N1**, you'll need to provide specific information, such as your name and address, the defendant's details, the amount you're claiming, and the reason for the claim. In addition to the claim form, you will need to attach any **supporting documents** that back up your case. This might include contracts, invoices, medical reports, or a Statement of Claim, which explains the reasons for your claim and the amount you're seeking.

 Once your claim form and documents are ready, you'll need to pay the court fee, which varies depending on the value of your claim. The fee structure is available at **https://www.gov.uk/make-court-claim-for-money/court-fees**.

---

44 https://www.gov.uk/government/publications/
    form-n1-claim-form-cpr-part-7

If you're financially eligible, you may be able to apply for a fee remission to reduce or waive the court fees.

With everything in order, you can **submit your claim**. If you're filing online, you'll submit the claim through the respective portal. For claims using Form N1, you'll send the completed form, along with your documents and payment, to the **Civil National Business Centre.** After you've filed your claim, the court will serve the claim on the defendant, who has a set period—usually **14 to 28 days**—to respond. If the defendant does not respond within this timeframe, the court may automatically rule in your favor. If the defendant contests the claim, a **hearing** will be scheduled, where both parties will present their evidence, and a judge will make a decision.

This process can be complex but knowing the steps to take and the forms to use helps streamline the claim. If you're unsure about any part of the process, it's recommended to **seek legal advice** to ensure your claim is filed properly.

Service of Documents

Understanding how documents are served in the UK is essential for anyone involved in legal proceedings, whether they are filing a claim or responding to one. The service of documents is governed by a set of legal rules designed to ensure that parties are properly notified of legal actions and proceedings. The primary framework for these rules falls under the **Civil Procedure Rules** (CPR), which outlines how service should be conducted.[45] According to these rules, when serving documents, the party responsible must adhere to specific requirements to ensure fairness and transparency throughout the legal process.

There are **different methods** of serving documents, depending on the situation and the parties involved. The most common methods include **personal service**, where documents are physically handed to the individual, and postal service, often using **first-class mail**, which allows for

---

45 https://maint.loc.gov/law/help/service-of-process/england.php

quicker delivery. Additionally, electronic methods such as email or fax can be used if both parties have agreed to accept service in these ways beforehand. Furthermore, for more urgent matters or when the recipient is untraceable, the court might authorize **alternative methods of service**. For example, documents could be sent via social media platforms like WhatsApp if the other party has been previously contacted that way, demonstrating a willingness to communicate through such channels.[46]

When it comes to who is responsible for serving the documents, it typically depends on the context of the case. In many instances, it is the claimant or their legal representative who must serve the documents. However, the court can also take on this responsibility if specified by the rules or practice directions. Aside from lawyers, other officials such as bailiffs or process servers may be tasked with delivering legal documents, particularly in situations where personal service is a requirement.

The service process follows a **few essential steps**. First, the documents that need to be served must be prepared and properly formatted according to court rules. Then, the chosen method of service should be executed—whether that is sending the documents by mail, handing them over in person, or using an electronic method. It's also important to ensure that the person receiving the documents is properly identified. After serving the documents, the server should document the details of the service, noting the time, method, and recipient, which leads us to how proof of service is documented.

Proof of service is a critical component of the legal process. Once the documents have been served, the individual or entity responsible must provide evidence that this has been completed. This is typically achieved by completing a document known as the **"certificate of service"** (Form N215), which details what was served, to whom it was served, and when and how the service occurred. In cases where documents are served personally, a statement confirming the details of the service should be made, and this certificate must be filed with the court to create an official record of service.

---

46 https://www.burnetts.co.uk/legal-news/
    the-right-and-wrong-way-to-serve-court-documents/

Statute of Limitations

Filing a civil suit in the UK is subject to certain deadlines, known as the statute of limitations. Essentially, this law sets time limits on how long someone has to initiate legal action after an incident occurs. Once the limitation period expires, the right to pursue the claim is typically lost, which means no court will hear the case, regardless of its merits. In the UK, different types of civil claims have specific time limits which vary depending on the nature of the claim.

For example, most **contract claims** must be filed within **six years** of the date of the breach. This means if someone fails to uphold their end of a contract, the other party has six years to take action against them. The same six-year limit generally applies to tort claims, which include **personal injury cases** or disputes related to **property damage**. However, personal injury claims, specifically, have a slightly different standard when it comes to knowing when the time limit begins. These claims must typically be initiated within three years from the date of the injury or from when the injured party became aware of the injury. This rule helps to accommodate situations where injuries may take time to manifest, such as in cases of medical negligence or workplace injuries.

It's also important to highlight that there are cases with **longer limitation periods**, such as actions related to **defective products** or disputes concerning **construction claims**, which can often have limitation periods of **up to 15 years** from the date the fault becomes apparent. This latter provision acknowledges that some problems, particularly in construction, may take a significant amount of time to surface after work is completed.

Several factors can also affect the length of the statute of limitations. For instance, the age and mental capacity of the claimant play a crucial role. If a claimant is under the age of 18 or mentally incapacitated at the time the claim arises, the limitation period does not start until they reach capacity by either turning 18 or regaining their mental capacity. Furthermore, if the responsible party has deliberately concealed relevant facts, the limitation period may not start until the claimant discovers or ought to have discovered those facts. These considerations help ensure that those who might need more time to act on a claim aren't unfairly disadvantaged.

If a civil suit is filed after the statute of limitations has **expired**, the defendant can raise this as a defense, often leading to the automatic dismissal of the claim. Essentially, even if the claim is valid and has merit, the court will not hear it if the time limit set by the statute has elapsed. This underscores the importance of being aware of the timelines involved and filing claims timely.

However, there are some **exceptions** that could potentially **extend** the statute of limitations. For instance, if **fraud** is involved, the limitation period may not start until the claimant discovers the fraud. This means that, in such cases, the law provides a mechanism to ensure that those who fail to disclose their wrongdoing cannot benefit from their deceit. Additionally, courts hold discretion under certain types of claims to extend or disapply the limitation periods to uphold justice, particularly in personal injury cases, where the court may allow more time if it is deemed fair to do so.

 ## Getting Married in the UK

Getting married in the UK involves a clear legal process with specific requirements for both British citizens and foreign nationals. The **legal requirements** for getting married in the UK include both parties being **at least 16 years old**, though if one or both individuals are aged between 16 and 18, **parental consent** is needed. In addition, the individuals must not be closely related, such as siblings or half-siblings, and they must be free to marry, meaning they aren't already married or in a civil partnership.

To **apply for a marriage license**, couples need to gather a few important documents. These include proof of identity, proof of nationality (such as a passport), and evidence of residence. If either person is divorced or widowed, they must provide a decree absolute or a death certificate, respectively. Non-English documents may need to be translated. In some cases, individuals may need to provide proof of their immigration status, especially if they are foreign nationals. Couples must first give **notice** of their **intention to marry** at a local registry office. This notice is typically given **at least 28 days before** the wedding date, and both parties must attend the registry office in person. The notice process ensures that no legal obstacles to the marriage exist. If either party is a foreign national, they may need to attend the registry office for an interview. If one or both parties are not British citizens or settled in the UK, the process may take longer due to additional checks.

For **foreign nationals**, there are specific **residency requirements**. If you are a foreign national wishing to marry in the UK, you must be living in the country for at least seven days before you give notice of your intention to marry. Some non-UK nationals may also need to apply for a visa, depending on their nationality and immigration status.

Couples can choose between a **civil ceremony** or a **religious ceremony**. For a civil ceremony, you'll marry at a registry office or approved venue, with a registrar conducting the ceremony. Civil ceremonies are legally binding and do not require religious content. A **religious ceremony**, on the other hand, can take place in a church, mosque, synagogue, or other places of worship. However, a religious marriage must also be registered by an authorized person, such as a priest or religious official, for it to be legally valid.

The **fees for getting married** can vary. For a civil ceremony at a registry office, the cost typically ranges from **£40 to £100** (**about US$45 to $110**), depending on the location and day of the week. If you marry at an approved venue, the costs can be higher, with prices starting from around **£200** (**about US$220**). Religious ceremonies are usually free, but fees may apply for administration and registration. There are also additional fees for obtaining a marriage certificate after the ceremony.

Once married, your **marriage is registered** with the local registry office. You will receive a marriage certificate as proof of your legal marriage, which can be used for various purposes, such as changing your name, applying for visas, or claiming tax benefits. The UK generally recognizes marriages conducted abroad, provided they meet the legal requirements of the country where the marriage took place. However, foreign nationals should check the specific rules of their home country regarding the recognition of UK marriages.

 **Law of the Land Hypothetical**

HYPOTHETICAL: *Joe, a tourist from the United States, was on holiday in the UK when he slipped and fell in a supermarket due to a wet floor that was not properly marked with a warning sign. Joe sustained a broken wrist and has incurred medical costs, along with lost wages from time off work. Can Joe, as a foreign visitor, file a personal injury claim in the UK for his accident, and what steps should he take to pursue compensation?*

ANSWER: *Yes. Joe, as a visitor to the UK, has the same rights to file a personal injury claim as a UK resident. The first step is ensuring medical treatment and gathering evidence, such as photos, medical reports, and witness statements. He should report the incident to the supermarket management as well. Joe has three years from the accident to file a claim, submitting it to the court. He can claim general damages for pain and suffering and special damages for medical costs and lost wages. If the supermarket is insured, the claim would go against their insurance; if not, Joe may use his own travel insurance. Joe should consider getting legal advice to guide him through the process.*

CHAPTER 25
OTHER THINGS TO KNOW

IN THIS CHAPTER

- Tourists and Street Hustling
- Safety Concerns and Practical Tips
- In the Event of Death
- Experiencing Financial Hardship

CHAPTER 25
OTHER THINGS TO KNOW

Tourists and Street Hustling

In the UK, street hustling is most commonly found in areas that attract large numbers of tourists. Major cities like **London, Edinburgh, Manchester**, and **Birmingham** are frequent hotspots, particularly in popular tourist districts. Locations such as **Covent Garden, Oxford Street, Leicester Square**, and **Piccadilly Circus** in London, as well as areas near famous landmarks like **Big Ben**, the **London Eye, Edinburgh Castle**, and the **Royal Mile** are particularly vulnerable. Transport hubs like **Victoria Station, King's Cross**, and **Heathrow Airport** are also places where tourists often encounter hustlers, as they may be less familiar with the area and thus more susceptible to scams.

Some common scams that tourists should watch out for include:

- **The Charity Scam:** Tourists are approached by individuals pretending to collect money for a charity, often with a clipboard in hand and a sob story about a worthy cause. In reality, the charity doesn't exist, and the money goes straight into the scammer's pocket.

- **Fake Petition Scams:** Hustlers often set up a "petition" in busy tourist spots, asking people to sign a cause-related petition (such as one for children's rights or animal welfare). Once the tourist signs it, the scammer may aggressively demand a donation, claiming it's for the cause listed on the petition.

- **The Friendship Bracelet Scam:** Tourists, especially in places like Covent Garden, are approached by individuals offering to tie "free" friendship bracelets on their wrists. Once the bracelet is tied, the scammer demands money, often asking for an exaggerated amount, claiming the bracelet is "free" but requires payment for their "time and effort."

- **Street Performers or Beggars:** Some performers or beggars may start with a dramatic performance, such as playing a musical instrument, singing, or telling an emotional story of hardship. After the performance, they may demand money, even though the tourist wasn't aware that they were expected to pay in the first place.

- **Overcharging:** In some busy tourist areas, street vendors, food trucks, or even taxi drivers may take advantage of tourists by charging inflated prices for goods or services. For instance, a taxi might take a longer route than necessary or offer a fare that's far higher than the local rate.

- **The Shell Game:** This is a more old-fashioned scam still occasionally seen in busy public areas. The hustler uses three cups and a small object, such as a coin, and tries to make tourists believe they can guess under which cup the coin is hidden. The scammer always wins and may pressure the tourist into betting money.

Local authorities and tourism organizations tackle street hustling through various measures. In high-risk areas, police increase patrols and surveillance to deter scammers, while designated officers or community wardens focus on preventing fraud in popular tourist districts like Covent Garden and Oxford Street.

Public information campaigns, including posters, signs, and leaflets, are placed in busy areas and transport hubs to educate tourists about common scams and prevention tips. Websites like VisitBritain also offer resources on spotting scams and what to do if targeted. Tourism groups work with local businesses and street performers to enforce ethical standards, such as requiring busking permits and clear pricing for vendors. Additionally, the UK enforces laws against anti-social behavior, allowing authorities to fine or remove those engaging in aggressive hustling.

Safety Concerns and Practical Tips

Interactions with street hustlers in the UK can pose several safety concerns. Tourists may be vulnerable to **emotional manipulation, distraction techniques**, or **financial scams**. In some cases, aggressive hustlers can create confrontational situations that escalate quickly, leaving tourists feeling intimidated or unsafe. While most street hustlers don't resort to physical violence, their tactics can be distressing, especially for those who are unfamiliar with such behaviors.

To protect themselves from aggressive hustlers, tourists should be cautious when approached by strangers, especially in busy tourist areas. It's advisable to **keep personal belongings secure** and **avoid engaging** with anyone who appears overly persistent or insistent. If confronted, staying calm and politely refusing to participate in any transaction can defuse many situations. Tourists should also trust their instincts. If a situation feels off, walking away or seeking help from a nearby shop or police officer can be the best option.

Local customs and behaviors can help tourists navigate street interactions more safely. In the UK, people generally value personal space, so if someone gets too close or seems intrusive, it's acceptable to step back or assert boundaries. Most locals will avoid engaging with street hustlers, and tourists can follow suit by remaining distant and avoiding eye contact. Additionally, keeping **interactions brief and polite** without making commitments or handing over money can minimize the risk of being targeted.

If tourists experience harassment or scams, several resources are available to report such incidents. The UK police offer **non-emergency reporting through 101**, where tourists can alert authorities about street hustlers or suspicious activity. Many tourist areas also have **local tourist information centers** where tourists can seek advice and report scams. Websites like **Action Fraud** (the UK's national fraud and cybercrime reporting center) provide an online platform to report fraud or scams. Additionally, some local councils may have dedicated street safety officers or hotlines for reporting harassment or aggressive begging.

 **In the Event of Death**

If someone traveling with you dies while in the UK, the situation can be overwhelming, but it's essential to follow a clear set of steps to handle the matter appropriately.

First, **contact local emergency services** by dialing **999**. This is the UK's emergency number, and they will dispatch medical or police help. If the death is sudden or occurs in a public place, police will likely need to be involved to determine the cause of death. If the death occurs in a hospital or medical facility, they will also guide you through the necessary steps.

Once emergency services have been contacted and the situation is under control, the next step is to **inform the relevant embassy or consulate**. The embassy or consulate of the deceased's home country can assist with legal and practical matters, including arranging for the body to be repatriated, offering consular support, and helping with the paperwork required for the death. They may also help notify family members back home.

Handling the **deceased's remains** involves a few legal steps. A medical certificate of death will be issued, which is necessary for funeral arrangements. In some cases, if the cause of death is unclear or suspicious, a post-mortem (autopsy) might be required by the coroner. This process can delay the release of the body but is part of the legal requirements in the UK. A local funeral director will guide you through the process of preparing for the funeral or repatriation, including obtaining a burial or cremation certificate.

If the family wishes to bring the body home, the funeral director can assist with the repatriation process. There are **several requirements**, including obtaining the necessary documentation, embalming the body, and arranging transportation with a specialized funeral service. The embassy or consulate can also help coordinate with the family, ensuring that all necessary paperwork is in place for both UK and international travel.

Families should be prepared for the costs involved in repatriating a body, as this can be expensive, and travel insurance may cover some of these expenses. If the deceased did not have insurance, it may be necessary to cover the costs out-of-pocket or seek assistance from the embassy, which may be able to direct families to resources or charity organizations that can offer help.

Experiencing Financial Hardship

Tourists in the UK might face financial hardship for a variety of reasons, such as unexpected medical emergencies, losing access to funds due to lost or stolen cards, poor exchange rates, or overspending during their trip. Currency fluctuations and high living costs in major cities like London can also cause budgeting challenges. While the UK is a popular destination, it can also be an expensive one, especially when factoring in transport, meals, and attractions.

If a tourist runs out of money or faces a financial emergency, the first step should be to **contact their bank or credit card** provider to block lost or stolen cards and inquire about emergency funds or alternatives. If this isn't possible, tourists can turn to their **embassy or consulate**, which can provide guidance and sometimes offer loans or financial assistance to cover basic expenses or repatriation costs.

There are also several **local resources** that may be able to help tourists facing financial difficulties. Some charities, such as The Salvation Army and local branches of the Red Cross, may provide support in cases of extreme hardship. Additionally, some hostels and hotels might offer emergency accommodations or allow delayed payments in difficult situations.

Understanding local costs and currency is crucial for avoiding financial issues. The UK uses the British pound (GBP), and tourists should be aware of exchange rates and any associated fees when converting money. Cash payments are common in some areas, while credit and debit cards are widely accepted. It's helpful to carry a small amount of cash for emergencies but rely on cards for larger purchases. Avoid relying solely on ATMs, as fees for withdrawals can add up, especially in tourist-heavy areas.

For budgeting, tourists can plan ahead by researching the costs of transportation, meals, and activities before their trip. Using budget apps and tracking spending throughout the trip can help keep expenses in check. Many UK cities offer discounts for public transportation and cultural attractions for students or tourists, so it's worth asking about any available deals. Additionally, self-catering accommodations, such as renting apartments or using hostel kitchens, can save on food costs.

CHAPTER 26
QUICK REFERENCE GUIDE

■ Quick Chapter References to Important Topics

QUICK REFERENCE GUIDE

Crime in the UK

Are there particular areas I should avoid as a tourist?

Yes. While the UK is generally safe for tourists, some areas require extra caution due to higher crime rates. In London, neighborhoods like Tottenham, Hackney, and Brixton can have higher street crime, though they offer cultural attractions. In Manchester, areas like Moss Side and Harpurhey see more crime, while in Birmingham, places like Handsworth and Nechells may be best avoided, especially at night. Liverpool's Anfield, Kirkdale, and Toxteth areas are also higher risk. In Nottingham, neighborhoods like St Ann's and Mapperley can be problematic. It's advisable to stay alert, avoid poorly lit areas at night, and use licensed taxis or rideshares for added safety. *For more details, see Chapter 3.*

Drug Offenses

Is the possession of marijuana legal?

No. The possession of marijuana is illegal in the UK. It is classified as a **Class B** drug under the **Misuse of Drugs Act 1971**. Possessing marijuana can lead to up to five years in prison, an unlimited fine, or both. While the police may issue a warning or penalty notice in some cases, possession remains an offense, and individuals can still be arrested.

Is the possession of cocaine legal?

No. The possession of cocaine is illegal in the UK. It is classified as a **Class A** drug under the **Misuse of Drugs Act 1971**, which carries severe penalties. Possession of cocaine can lead to up to seven years in prison, an unlimited fine, or both. Dealing or trafficking cocaine can result in sentences ranging from 25 years to life imprisonment. *For more details, see Chapter 4.*

Alcohol-Related Offenses

What is the legal drinking age?

In the UK, the **legal drinking age is 18**. Individuals must be at least 18 years old to purchase alcohol in shops, bars, and restaurants.

What is the legal blood alcohol limit to drive?

The legal blood alcohol limit in the UK varies by county. In England, Wales, and Northern Ireland, the limit is 0.80 grams of alcohol per 100 milliliters of blood. In Scotland, the limit is lower at 0.50 grams per 100 milliliters of blood.

Drivers caught with a blood alcohol level over the limit can face fines, driving bans, or imprisonment, depending on the severity of the offense. *For more details, see Chapter 5.*

Firearm & Ammunition Offenses

Can I possess a gun?

Yes. In the UK, the possession of a gun is highly regulated. Generally, it is illegal to possess a firearm without the proper licensing. To own a firearm legally, individuals must apply for a firearm certificate (FAC) or shotgun certificate (SGC), which are issued by the police. The process involves background checks, proving a valid reason for ownership (such as hunting or sport shooting), and ensuring that the firearm is stored securely. Without these licenses, possessing a gun is illegal, and penalties can include imprisonment.

Can I possess ammunition?

Yes. Possessing ammunition in the UK is also regulated. To own ammunition, you must have a valid firearm or shotgun certificate. It is illegal to possess ammunition for a firearm you do not have a certificate for, and unauthorized possession can lead to serious legal consequences. However, if you have a valid certificate, you are allowed to possess ammunition in the quantities and types approved on your certificate. *For more details, see Chapter 6.*

Prostitution

Is prostitution legal?

Yes. Prostitution itself is legal in the UK, but related activities like soliciting in public, running a brothel, or pimping are illegal. Selling sex privately between consenting adults is allowed, but exploitation and coercion are prohibited. *For more details, see Chapter 7.*

LGBTQ

Is homosexuality legal?

Yes. Homosexuality is legal in the UK. The country decriminalized homosexual acts between consenting adults in 1967, and same-sex couples have the same legal rights as heterosexual couples.

Are same-sex public displays of affection legal?

Yes. Same-sex public displays of affection are legal in the UK. There are no laws prohibiting same-sex couples from showing affection in public, and they are protected under the same anti-discrimination laws as heterosexual couples. *For more details, see Chapter 8.*

Arrested in the UK

Would I be entitled to bail if I'm arrested?

In the UK, whether or not you are entitled to bail depends on the nature of the offense you have been arrested for. Generally, you may be granted bail unless the police or the courts believe that there is a risk you might abscond, commit further offenses, or interfere with evidence or witnesses. Bail can be granted by the police or by the courts, and there are conditions that may be attached to it.

Will a lawyer be provided to me if I cannot afford one?

Yes. If you cannot afford a lawyer in the UK, you may be entitled to legal representation through legal aid, provided you meet certain criteria. Legal aid is available for individuals who cannot afford to pay for a lawyer, and it covers various stages of legal proceedings, including police interviews and court hearings. Eligibility depends on factors like income, the seriousness of the case, and the chances of success in the case. If you're eligible, you will be appointed a lawyer who will represent you at no cost or at a reduced fee. *For more details, see Chapter 10.*

Helping a Friend or Relative Imprisoned in the UK

Can I send money to a friend or relative imprisoned in the UK?

Yes. You can send money to a friend or family member who is imprisoned in the UK. However, the process for doing so varies depending on the prison. You will typically need to use a system set up by the UK prison service, such as sending money via a secure payment service. It is important to check with the specific prison for details on how to send money, as each facility may have different rules or platforms in place.

Can I remain in the UK upon release from prison or jail after my sentence is complete?

If you are a foreign national, you may not automatically be allowed to remain in the UK after completing your prison sentence. Upon release, the UK authorities may assess your immigration status. If you have no legal right to stay in the country (for example, if your visa has expired or if you were in the UK unlawfully), you could be detained for deportation. However, if you are a citizen or have legal residency, you may be able to remain in the UK after serving your sentence. *For more details, see Chapter 12.*

Crime Victim Assistance

Can a victim of a crime be legally compensated?

Yes. A victim of a crime in the UK can be legally compensated through the Criminal Injuries Compensation Scheme (CICS). This government program provides financial compensation to individuals who suffer physical or psychological injury as a result of violent crime. The compensation can cover medical expenses, lost earnings, pain and suffering, and other costs incurred as a result of the crime. The victim must apply within two years of the crime taking place, though there are exceptions in some cases.

How can a foreigner in the UK report a crime they are a victim of?

A foreigner in the UK can report a crime by calling **999** for emergencies or **101** for non-urgent situations. Police can arrange interpreters if needed. Online reporting is available for some crimes, such as fraud. Additionally, the embassy or consulate can assist in reporting the crime and provide support with language or legal rights. *For more details, see Chapter 14.*

U.S. Consulate Assistance

Are there any limitations to the consulate assistance I can receive while in the UK?

Yes. There are limitations to consulate assistance in the UK. While consulates can offer help with legal issues, emergencies, and contacting family, they cannot intervene in local legal matters, such as representing you in court or preventing you from being prosecuted under UK law. They also cannot provide financial aid for personal expenses or bail, though they may assist in arranging funds from family or friends. *For more details, see Chapter 14.*

Police

Is there an official police force?

Yes. The UK has an official police force, which is made up of multiple regional and national police services. The most well-known is the **Metropolitan Police Service** (**MPS**), which is responsible for law enforcement in Greater London (excluding the City of London). Other areas of the UK, such as Scotland and Wales, have their own police forces, including **Police Scotland** and **North Wales Police**. The UK also has specialized forces like the **British Transport Police** for transport-related matters and the **National Crime Agency** (**NCA**) for tackling serious and organized crime. Each police force operates under the law and is responsible for maintaining public safety, investigating crimes, and enforcing laws. *For more details, see Chapter 15.*

How to Get Legal Help in the UK

Is there a resource in the UK to find legal representation?

Yes. There are resources in the UK to find legal representation. The Law Society offers a "Find a Solicitor" service, which allows individuals to search for solicitors by area of law and location. Additionally, the Citizens Advice Bureau can provide guidance on finding legal help.

Is there free legal representation assistance?

Yes. In the UK, free legal representation may be available in some situations through Legal Aid. Legal Aid is a government program designed to provide assistance to individuals who cannot afford legal representation, but it is typically only available for cases related to serious criminal matters, family law issues, or housing problems. Eligibility for Legal Aid depends on your income, savings, and the type of case you're involved in. *For more details, see Chapter 16.*

Foreign Embassies in the UK

Are there foreign embassies in the UK?

Yes. There are foreign embassies in the UK. London, the capital of the United Kingdom, hosts a large number of embassies from countries around the world. These embassies provide a range of services for their nationals, including consular support, visa services, and assistance in emergencies.

Is there a website to locate embassies in the UK?

Yes. To locate embassies in the UK, you can visit the official UK Government website at **https://www.gov.uk/world/embassies**. This website offers a comprehensive list of foreign embassies, consulates, and high commissions in the UK, with contact details, locations, and information on the services they provide. *For more details, see Chapter 16.*

Medical Facilities & Hospitals

Is there a number I can call for ambulance and fire emergencies?

Yes. In the UK, you can call **999** for ambulance, fire, or any emergency service. This is the official emergency number, and it can be dialed free of charge from any phone.

If I am injured while on vacation in the UK, are there hospitals that are recommended for tourists?

If you're injured while on vacation in the UK, there are no specific hospitals exclusively for tourists, but all NHS (National Health Service) hospitals provide care to anyone, regardless of nationality. Major cities, such as London, Manchester, and Edinburgh, have well-equipped hospitals that are experienced in treating tourists. Many hospitals in the UK also offer emergency care and have Accident & Emergency (A&E) departments that operate 24/7. *For more details, see Chapter 17.*

Driving in the UK

Which side of the road do I drive on?

In the UK, you drive on the **left side** of the road. The steering wheel in cars is also on the right-hand side.

Can I use my driver's license from my home country to drive in the UK?

Yes. You can use your **driver's license from your home country** to drive in the UK for up to **12 months**. However, if you're planning to stay longer, you may need to exchange your foreign license for a UK one.

How old do I need to be to rent a car?

To rent a car in the UK, the minimum age is typically **21**, but this can vary depending on the rental company. Some companies may charge an additional fee for drivers under 25, and others may require you to have held your license for a certain period (usually at least one year). Always check the rental company's policy for specific age restrictions and conditions. *For more details, see Chapter 18.*

Nude Beaches & Clothing-Optional Resorts

Is public nudity legal on the beaches?

No. In the UK, public nudity is generally not allowed except on designated nudist beaches, where it is legal. Outside these areas, public nudity may lead to charges of outraging public decency. Always check for specific locations where nudity is permitted. *For more details, see Chapter 19.*

Tourist Taxation

Is there room tax in the UK?

In the UK, there is **no specific room tax** for hotel stays, but a **Value Added Tax (VAT)** of 20 percent is usually included in the price of accommodations. Some regions may charge additional fees, like **tourism levies**, but this varies.

Is there any fee associated with leaving the UK?

No. There is no fee for leaving the UK. However, airports and transport hubs might charge extra for certain services or amenities, but there are no exit taxes or charges for simply departing the country. *For more details, see Chapter 22.*

Long-Term Stays

Do I need to return to my home country to apply for a work permit in the UK?

No. As an American citizen, you **do not need to return to your home country** to apply for a work permit in the UK. You can apply for a work visa from within the UK if you meet the eligibility requirements. However, you must have a valid job offer from a licensed sponsor, and the job must meet specific criteria.

As an American, how long can I stay in the UK without a visa?

Americans can stay for up to six months as a tourist or for business purposes without a visa. However, this does not allow you to work or engage in activities that require a work permit. If you wish to work, study, or engage in other activities, you will need to apply for the appropriate visa before or during your stay. *For more details, see Chapter 23.*

In the Event of Death

What documents would an embassy need regarding the death of a tourist?

If a tourist dies in the UK, the embassy typically requires several documents to assist with the process. These include the death certificate issued by UK authorities, the deceased's passport for identity verification, and a consular report of death. The embassy will also need contact details for the next of kin and proof of their relationship, such as a birth or marriage certificate. Medical records, an autopsy report, and a police report (if applicable) may also be required, especially if the death was accidental or suspicious. Additionally, information about travel insurance or funeral arrangements will help with repatriation and other logistical matters. *For more details, see Chapter 25.*

EMERGENCY/IMPORTANT CONTACT NUMBERS IN THE UK

 Please consider putting some of these numbers in your phone prior to traveling to the UK.

Emergency Numbers:

- **Police:** 999 or 112
- **Fire:** 999 or 112
- **Ambulance:** 999 or 112

Other Useful Contacts:

- **NHS:** 111
- **Coast Guard:** 999 or 112 (ask for Coastguard)
- **Roadside Assistance:** The AA (Automobile Association) - 0800 88 77 66; RAC - 0330 159 1111

Legal Assistance:

- **The Bar Council:** 020 7222 2555
- **Legal Aid:** Citizens Advice - 03444 111 444 or visit www.citizensad-vice.org.uk for free legal advice.

USEFUL BRITISH PHRASES

 These casual colloquial phrases will help you blend in and understand local conversations, making your trip to the UK feel more authentic!

"FANCY A CUPPA?" – Would you like a cup of tea?

"I'M KNACKERED." – I'm very tired.

"IT'S ALL GONE PEAR-SHAPED." – Things have gone wrong.

"CHEERS!" – Thank you (or used when making a toast).

"I'M JUST POPPING TO THE LOO." – I'm just going to the bathroom.

"IT'S A DODDLE." – It's very easy.

"BLIMEY!" – An exclamation of surprise (similar to "Wow!" or "Goodness!").

"I'M CHUFFED." – I'm pleased or happy about something.

"THAT'S RUBBISH!" – That's nonsense or untrue.

"I'M OFF TO THE SHOPS." – I'm going to the store.

"I'M SKINT." – I'm broke (I don't have any money).

"WHAT'S THE DAMAGE?" – How much does it cost?

"IT'S A BIT DODGY." – It's a little suspicious or not quite right.

"PULL YOUR SOCKS UP." – Improve your behavior or performance.

"DON'T GET SHIRTY." – Don't get angry or upset.

"BOB'S YOUR UNCLE." – A phrase used to say "and there you go," meaning everything will be fine or simple.

GLOSSARY

ACQUITTAL: A jury verdict that a criminal defendant is not guilty, or the finding of a judge that the evidence cannot support a conviction.

ADVERSARY PROCEEDING: A lawsuit arising from a controversy that begins with filing a complaint.

AFFIDAVIT: A written statement made under oath.

APPEAL: A request made after a trial court has decided against one party in which the losing party asks a higher court to review the decision for legal error.

ARRAIGNMENT: A proceeding in which a criminal defendant is brought to court, told of the charges, and asked to plead guilty or not guilty.

BAIL: The temporary release of a person from jail when awaiting trial, on condition that a sum of money be lodged or deposited to guarantee an appearance in court.

BARRISTER: A lawyer admitted to plead at the Bar and who may try cases in superior court.

BURDEN OF PROOF: The duty to prove disputed facts.

CAUSE OF ACTION: A legal claim in a civil action.

COMPLAINT: A written statement that begins a civil lawsuit in which the plaintiff details the claims.

CONTRACT: An agreement between two or more persons to do something or to not do something.

CONVICTION: A judgment of guilt against a person charged with a crime.

CUSTOMS DUTY: A tariff or tax imposed on goods when transported across international borders.

COURT LIAISON: A person that coordinates with attorneys to perform administrative duties, such as scheduling witnesses, sharing information with law enforcement, and overseeing the reporting of cases to foreign embassies when applicable.

DAMAGES: Money that a defendant pays to a plaintiff in a civil case if the plaintiff wins.

DEFENDANT: 1) The individual against whom a civil claim is filed; 2) The individual against whom a criminal claim is filed.

FELONY: A serious crime, punishable by more than one year in prison.

MAGISTRATE: A judicial officer of a district court, who conducts initial proceedings in criminal cases, decides criminal misdemeanor cases, conducts many pretrial civil and criminal matters on behalf of district judges, and decides civil cases with the consent of the parties.

MISDEMEANOR: An offense punishable by one year or less in jail.

PLAINTIFF: A person or business that files a formal complaint with the court.

PLEA: In a criminal case, the answer of "guilty," "not guilty," or "no contest" in response to a criminal charge.

SOLICITOR: A lawyer who advises clients, represents them in lower court, and prepares cases for barristers to try in higher courts.

SOVEREIGN IMMUNITY: A legal doctrine by which the sovereign or the state (i.e. government) cannot commit a legal wrong and thus, it is immune from criminal and civil liability and cannot be sued.

STATUTE: A written law passed by a legislative body.

STATUTE OF LIMITATIONS: A statute prescribing a period of limitation to bring certain types of legal actions. If the action is not brought within that time, the person or entity (in a criminal context) is permanently barred from suing in court.

SUBPOENA: A command, issued under court authority, for a witness to appear and to give testimony.

TESTIMONY: Evidence presented orally by witnesses.

VERDICT: The decision of a judge or jury in a case.

WARRANT: Court authorization to conduct a search or to make an arrest.

ACKNOWLEDGMENTS

This book series would never have seen the light of day without the able assistance of the following people:

Kathy Adams, my paralegal for over 22 years, who is the "Best" I've ever worked with during my entire legal career because of her amazing work ethic, organizational skills, and her ability to think outside of the box in unique and creative ways;

Ally Knez-Siddique, a professional writer, and one of my paralegals, whose eye for detail, according to her, is both a blessing and a curse;

Gino Ibanez, my former law clerk, whose exceptional research skills helped move this book series along in its early stages;

Rosa Diaz Graham, my legal assistant who helped with research and word processing at the very beginning of this project;

Shelia Martin, one of my former paralegals, worked diligently on this series of books, even after taking on another job. Her organizational skills are reflected throughout;

Mindy Scarlett, my marketing and publishing "Guru"! Her creativity and vision have no boundaries!

ABOUT THE AUTHOR

Michael L. Moore practices in Orlando, Florida, the city where he spent his formative years. He credits the trauma of having his brother murdered when he was only 10 years old, as the catalyst that drew him into the practice of law.

Moore attended Florida State University, where he was a member of the FSU debate team. Upon graduating, he was awarded a full scholarship to attend the University of Tennessee College of Law, where he was elected President of the Student Bar Association. He further honed his advocacy and public speaking skills by participating in 'moot court' competitions.

After clerking at the Tennessee Attorney General's office while in law school, Moore moved back to Orlando, Florida, to work at the State Attorney's Office as a prosecutor, and where he was fortunate enough to meet the young lady that would eventually become his wife. Moore moved on to working for private law firms, both local and national, and eventually established his own law firm in 1999. He continues to make Orlando his home base.

It was the murder of a close friend and client in Jamaica that caused Moore to realize that books on laws in other countries were few and far between, and he was inspired to create Law of the Land Publishing. Moore launched Law of the Land Publishing to provide a series of guidebooks and a membership site for tourists and business travelers to stay up to date on the laws in each country they travel to, as well as having access to assistance if they run into legal issues.

"My vision is to educate people on what their legal rights are, and how they can access legal assistance, no matter where they have to travel to in the world," said Moore. "As Americans, we have a right to due process, but in some countries, you don't even have the right to access a square meal when incarcerated. My goal is to provide the information needed to stay out of trouble, as well as having access to assistance if trouble finds you."

www.ingramcontent.com/pod-product-compliance
Lightning Source LLC
Chambersburg PA
CBHW070913120626
46546CB00001B/245